D1468908

ALSO AVAILABLE

MASTERS AT WORK

BECOMING A RESTAURATEUR

PATRIC KUH

SIMON & SCHUSTER

New York   London   Toronto   Sydney   New Delhi

Simon & Schuster
1230 Avenue of the Americas
New York, NY 10020

First Simon & Schuster hardcover edition May 2019

For information about special discounts for bulk purchases,
please contact Simon & Schuster Special Sales at 1-866-506-1949
or business@simonandschuster.com.

The Simon & Schuster Speakers Bureau can bring authors to your
live event. For more information or to book an event, contact the
Simon & Schuster Speakers Bureau at 1-866-248-3049
or visit our website at www.simonspeakers.com.

Interior design by Jennifer K. Beal Davis

Manufactured in the United States of America

1 3 5 7 9 10 8 6 4 2

Library of Congress Cataloging-in-Publication Data has been applied for.

ISBN 978-1-9821-0330-9
ISBN 978-1-9821-0331-6 (ebook)

To my friend, Alain Giraud.

CONTENTS

BECOMING

A

RESTAURATEUR

1

VISIONARY

Even though it's a midweek night, there's a buzzy feel to the dining room at Here's Looking at You, one of the best restaurants in Los Angeles. If you stepped inside, you'd hear conversations pierced by laughter at the twelve tables and packed bar. You'd see one group of six excitedly pass around handmade bowls of Carolina Gold rice topped with a crisp wafer of parsley-flecked crackling chicken skin. When they taste it, they nod in agreement. It's that good.

When Lien Ta, the restaurateur who launched the restaurant in 2016, moves about the dining room, she notices other things. She wishes one table had moved on to dessert, but their dinner has yet to be cleared. But hey, over there a couple is drinking two of the newly launched cocktails, so those seem to be working. Grabbing a napkin from the bar, she bends to pick up two shishito pepper stems on the floor. Seeing a man in a loosened tie, a semiregular who's joined a larger group, she waves, then greets him with a warm smile. And by name.

A good restaurant should feel as welcoming as someone's home. After all, restaurateurs see you as guests, not customers. Except a home isn't a business, with all the practical requirements of overhead and wages and reports. But Lien, like many other restaurateurs, knows that when the math of an evening has been calculated, what guests will remember most is how a place made them feel. Which is why her main focus is setting the right tone from the start. When the phone rings? She answers with enthusiasm. When a guest emails with a special event request to buy out the entire restaurant? She replies in such a way that propels them forward with their plans. And she has clear ideas of how she wants the guests greeted. Having checked the dining room, she moves quickly to join the new hostess at the narrow wood stand immediately inside the door.

Lien, for example, doesn't want her hostesses greeting single diners at her restaurant with the phrase "*Just* one?" She feels it sounds judgy. On a busy night, she'd rather book a 6 p.m. than a 6:30 p.m. reservation because she'll get the table back for a second turn at 8 p.m. She sets the time for slots herself—an hour and forty-five minutes for two, two hours for four. The online reservation system will never allow parties to overlap; it will always play it safe. Lien takes pains to make sure each guest feels welcomed at the start of the meal and relaxed through its conclusion. But a restaurateur's mission is to fill seats. This is LA; people will no-show. Because the Wiltern theater, a landmark sea-foam-green art deco tower, is nearby, some folks will actually arrive to their 6 p.m. reservation on time and eat quickly to make the show, so the table is free when the next group arrives at 8 p.m. But when that doesn't happen, the time for the next party's wait—referred to as the "quote time"—has to be delivered in an upbeat, positive way that makes people resolve a few minutes' wait is not a big deal. When things really start to drag, there's always the option of offering a drink on the house. Over and over again, Lien must balance guests' experiences with her financial reality.

That kind of constant balancing is what it takes to succeed in this demanding career. Here's the reality: It's high-risk. It's long hours. It can be bureaucratic hell. But at the end of the day, it is also deeply satisfying. No matter whether you get into the industry through a part-time summer job or with a degree in hospitality from a prestigious university, make sure that the business is right for you and that you're right for it.

Each staff member, for example, has a different (and highly specific) set of responsibilities, so it's no surprise that when

Lien trains a new hostess, she stands right beside her. The young woman at the stand tonight is on her third shift and has been doing well. She did not say "Just one?" to the solitary diner who happened in after exploring the neighborhood. Seeing another party was lingering, the hostess extended their stay—which meant that they were still seated when the next party tumbled out of an Uber in high spirits. Lien flashed a welcoming smile but stepped back to watch the tone, engagement, and sense of welcome the hostess extended. And she allowed herself a smile when the young woman quickly changed the seating chart, getting that party another table—a better table, in fact—that had opened up moments earlier.

Located one block north of Wilshire Boulevard, Here's Looking at You—or HLAY, as those who work there pronounce it—occupies the ground floor of a building on a corner of 6th Street just northeast of Wilshire and Western, two of LA's busier thoroughfares and an intersection that serves as the heart of what has become America's largest Koreatown. The restaurant sits among the neighborhood's soju joints, bulgogi halls, Paris-themed patisseries, and all-night steam saunas. It shares the ground floor with a barber, a sushi spot, and a modest general store. Above them is a second floor of offices. Early mixed-use? Hard to tell. Though far more modest than the nearby Wiltern theater, the structure shares a look with the classic building. The zigzag corners and moldings allude to more than embody the art deco style that was popular in LA in the 1930s. Over the years this same spot housed a locksmith with a key-cutting booth, a beauty parlor, and a psychic reader who left behind what is now HLAY's blue neon sign. The restaurant's name—inspired by the toast and a card in Lien's stationery collection—is painted nearby on the glass window in flowing gold script.

Lien and her business partner, chef Jonathan Whitener, opened HLAY in July of 2016. It has since gone on to represent one of the high points of the city's unaffected and wide-ranging dining style. Having been, respectively, the manager and chef of Animal, the Fairfax Avenue storefront that was a breakthrough success with its gleefully over-the-top flavors, Lien and Jonathan had instant name recognition in LA's food scene. But it also could have gone the wrong way. New restaurants tend to follow one of two possible patterns: They come out of the gate with every detail thought out, every interaction discussed in preshift and executed in service, the message totally focused—or, in hindsight, their early version was no more than a draft of what the restaurant will become. They need what the neighborhood and its customers bring to define themselves.

Three years after its opening, HLAY is the second kind of

restaurant, and it is stronger for it. The assembled midcentury Scandinavian-style furniture, the Morrissey portrait, the minimal look that early on felt almost reserved turns out to have been just right for a venture in an evolving neighborhood, where bone-broth halls and skater-gear stores were starting to coexist. Wearing their own clothes—a mix of floral patterns, jeans, and heavy cotton aprons—the staff looks approachable, warm, and, well, neighborly. Even having Jonathan's collection of cookbooks ranged in modular bookshelves above the bar and by the entrance kind of makes sense. You never know when you might want to take one down if the conversation turns to Paul Bocuse, the guardian of haute cuisine, or Michel Bras, the descendant who gave it a foraged overlay. Mexican-American on his mother's side, German-American on his father's, and a child of suburban Orange County, Jonathan is able to draw from a slew of cultures and frames them in hard-won technique.

"There are always signals in Jonathan's cooking," Lien says. Which means the spicy seasoning on the frog's legs may be a nod to the salt-and-pepper pork chops of a Chinese takeout menu, the dab of cool mayo on the tapioca fritters a wink to a Brazilian pairing he read about. Rigorous yet inviting, the restaurant soon started gathering accolades from online authorities and the national press. *Los Angeles* magazine named it one of its top ten new openings. Jonathan Gold, the longtime *Los Angeles Times* critic, praised the cognac swizzle served at the bar and the way the radish butter melted over the thirty-day dry-aged Holstein rib eye. More recently, a *New York Times* article on LA's evolving restaurant scene featured a large exterior photo of HLAY. "A reminder of the things that have always made this city so dynamic," noted *Food & Wine* in 2017 when placing the restaurant on its top ten national openings list.

Stepping away from the hostess stand, Lien moves between tables, a petite figure in an aubergine dress, fashionable white calf-length socks, and black leather ankle boots. While the critics debated the multifaceted inspiration behind Jonathan's cooking, it was Lien's choices that ensured their reviews of HLAY. Her job is a curious one: As a restaurateur, she must be proficient in many different skills. These include the ability to read leases and meet payroll, to see potential in individuals who may never have cooked or carried a dish before, to keep their spirits up in an industry of grinding hours, and to always be ready to adjust course in search of higher-quality food and service and better financial results. The term "restaurateur" also connotes a level of urbane ease that would prompt most actual restaurateurs to smile. Lien certainly does. "I can't bus tables very well," she says of the skill of carrying many plates gracefully. "And my method for running a tray of martinis," she says of the high-stemmed glasses that are so easy to spill, "is to find someone else to do it."

As Lien turns, a waiter walks out of the kitchen carrying a bowl of mackerel under a thatch of pickled Asian pear with kombu broth. Like the seating plan, every dish and every drink is part of its own financial equation that itself is a portion of the restaurant's financial health. The drinks artfully poured in tall etched glasses and tiki cups at the bar are part of an equation, too: Liquor is supposed to bring in 25 percent of the restaurant's revenue. Though all the bar seats are taken, they are not open seating because empty stools, the natural buffer people like to establish between themselves and others, mean less space and lost revenue. Lien or the hostess have led people to each one, the end result of a reservation that began with a pull-down option on the OpenTable site. "Our contractor found this zebra-patterned bamboo," Lien says, running her hand alongside the bar's edge as Harry, the chief barman, vigorously shakes a drink in a tin cup. "I just thought a wooden bar is a disaster because of all the water, but we went with it. What was shocking about all the trips to the lumberyard and the tile store was having to pay for it all. I know that sounds so naïve, but purchasing and paying for construction materials"—she pauses for effect—"is real."

At certain moments Lien has the ability both to be in total command of the restaurant's costs and to appear somewhat surprised by them. Financial smarts are central to her job, a skill that she has proven time and again. She took the lead in raising the $750,000 initially invested in the restaurant. She cut the checks for the visits to the lumberyard. And the tile store. And to Harry, the chief barman, and the waiter, and the new hostess. And to the California Department of Alcoholic Beverage Control. She and Jonathan pay back their investors regularly, and they're even in the beginning stages of raising money for a second restaurant.

From this vantage point, the difficulties of Lien's chosen profession momentarily come into focus. For all the anxiety that often pulses around a hostess stand on a busy night, crowded dining rooms can also be places of deep relaxation. Restaurants are the place we chose to impress, to celebrate, to reconnect, and, sometimes, to break up. Because of that, there are moments that almost glow with meaning. Lit by a centerpiece candle, the grandchild's head rests against her grandparent's shoulder, hands hold each other across a table, old friends lean in for another retelling of the infamous anecdote, the deal has been clinched, the declaration made, the happy birthday sung. These are the golden moments of restaurants. But they are made possible by budgets and staff training and more. It can seem like a strange thing, a restaurant, a riddle almost, a space that generates priceless memories *and* necessary income.

A few taps of the keys of her laptop at any moment would convert figures for the period, week, night, shift, and even the hour into columns, charts, or spreadsheets. Lien need only turn to the point-of-sale monitor near the bar, where servers punch in orders, to access the constantly changing sales figures for this evening. But in the restaurant business, metrics only say so much. For all these certainties, uncertainty is the order of the day; according to a 2005 Ohio State University study, 59 percent of restaurants fail within three years.

A few nights earlier, Lien attended a restaurant promotional event in a downtown loft space, and after handing out hundreds of food samples, she'd come away slightly shaken. "We live in a cocoon," she'd said. "Because people come to our restaurant, we think we're known. But none of these people have heard of us. We still haven't reached them." Now, scanning the room, she is in much the same kind of mood. Come tomorrow morning she'll be able to tell exactly how much business the bar and kitchen did, but not whether the guests who ordered enjoyed the experience. Or whether they'll be back.

2

FACILITATOR

Lien is thirty-seven, divorced, bubbly to the point that at Wheeler High in Marietta, Georgia, she was named homecoming and prom queen. It was editing the yearbook, though, that she credits with giving her a head for names— a priceless talent when greeting people at her restaurant's door. The South also gave her a sense of innate hospitality. She was a young girl when she arrived there. Her parents had left war-torn Vietnam by boat following the fall of Saigon and, after a year in a refugee camp in Thailand, had been sponsored by a church group to travel to the US. They landed in Kansas, then moved to San Francisco, where Lien was born, before moving to Southern California to operate a beauty salon and eventually to the suburbs of Atlanta. By then her father was ill; when he died, Lien, at age thirteen, ate in other people's homes while her mother grieved, starting a meaningful ritual she would continue for years after.

"I had a lot of amazing Southern families who adopted me for a couple of years," she recalls. "I did a lot of Thanksgivings and Christmases and strange suburban activities with awesome, wonderful families who cared for me and showed me how to behave at the dinner table."

She credits some of those meals as awakening in her a sense of the value of hospitality and the role restaurants play in creating genuine interactions and warmth. The technical education that would lead to those qualities becoming her actual profession was full of enough twists it might appear haphazard. But wherever she worked, she was always looking for ways to become more useful to daily operations. There are, however, more structured plans for individuals wishing to enter the profession, including part-time, online and four-year courses at community colleges, culinary institutes, and universities. With varying emphasis, each course covers the basics of finances, marketing, and organizational leadership (invariably requiring an internship) that give students confidence when they eventually begin their job search. Mastery, of course, takes time, long hours logged in a variety of positions, and a continuing desire to learn.

In Jonathan, a thirty-one-year-old with an eye for mid-century furniture at yard sales, Lien found a partner who in some ways is her opposite: She is five foot one, he is six foot five; she is sociable, he is given to solitary research that can result in dishes inspired by a mash-up of cultures and where the technique is so solid, it seems like the invisible but necessary component. But over the four years they've been business partners, Lien and Jonathan have grown into a team. Every restaurateur has a spark that moves things from the conceptual to the practical; for Lien, that spark was Jonathan.

They became friends over Vietnamese food. Or at least Jonathan's disbelief—and borderline annoyance—that she knew so little about it. He would mention *rau raum*, red perilla, or any of the herbs that contribute vital freshness to a steaming bowl of pho, and she would draw a blank. His knowledge wasn't from books, but from a childhood spent in Orange County, California. He grew up in Midway City, a tiny community that is crossed by Bolsa Avenue, one of the main thoroughfares of an enclave known as Little Saigon. Driving east from the 405 freeway off-ramp, the seemingly generic Southern California landscape suddenly gives way to a distant land. The red-and-yellow-striped flag that, decades after the war ended, still symbolizes South Vietnam flutters over cemeteries. Strip malls teem with open storefronts, where sardine banh mi sandwiches and diced yellow jackfruit—scooped into Ziploc bags—are for sale.

Lien's family fled Vietnam in boats, but her childhood was a place of American rituals. Even her name borders two cultures. It is spelled in a Vietnamese manner, but it is pronounced "Lynn," though in a lighthearted moment she might embellish it with a proper Southern purr. Jonathan didn't quite grow up in the Vietnamese world, but he was close enough to it that when pallets of Courvoisier landed on the supermarket floor, he knew it meant Tet, the New Year festival, was on its way. It wasn't preordained that Jonathan and Lien would go into partnership, but it would have been a shame had they not.

They met at Animal in February 2013. Jon Shook and Vinny Dotolo had come so close to winning *Iron Chef* in 2006 on the Food Network (they lost by a point) that they were able to open Animal in 2008 on Fairfax Avenue in LA. Located in the city's historic Jewish core, set amid Lubavitcher bookstores and fishmongers selling Riga sprats, Animal used bold flavors and unsung animal parts. Their big sellers were foie gras with biscuits and gravy, foie gras loco moco, and the foie gras sauce they poured over fries in a gonzo version of the Canadian trencher, poutine. Almost from the moment they were introduced, these hearty stoner-slash-Rabelaisian dishes could not be taken off the menu. At least not until California instituted a ban on the use of foie gras in July of 2012. "They were doing $1 million a year in foie gras," Jonathan remembers. And suddenly not.

Shook and Dotolo, who by then had opened Son of a Gun, a seafood restaurant about a mile away, moved their focus to catering and launching other ventures, leaving Jonathan in charge of Animal. Newly hired, he first put his imprint on the kitchen by insisting all the cooks wear uniforms. "When they promoted me, I was there forty-five-plus days straight because I trimmed the whole line. There were guys cooking in board shorts. I was like, this mentality is not going to work here. The kind of guy who's going to wear board shorts in my kitchen is not the guy who's going to produce good food. 'Do I have permission to change this?' 'Go for it.' I instituted uniforms, I was like, 'You guys can wear black pants, white porter shirts, and a blue apron. And have a hat on, please. Everyone has to be in uniform.' People were like, 'I quit. I'm not wearing a uniform here.' 'Bye.'"

Jonathan drew his crew tight around him. He was then in a perfect position to execute Shook and Dotolo's plan to make up for the foie gras shortfall by delving deeper into catering, a source of revenue that had always been central to their operation. But doing so meant having cooks for dinner service and catering working side by side. During the day, the bar counter and every inch of available table space became a cutting board. The corridors were lined with stacked Cambro coolers destined for events, lists of their contents taped to the hinged tops. When there was no room left in the restaurant's walk-in, Jonathan rented two refrigerated vans, which they kept humming parked in the alley by the back door. It was a grind that Lien, a manager with shifts split between Animal and Son of a Gun and still plenty of time to post her weekend activities on social media, didn't seem to share.

Just as the kitchen—the back of the house—has a hierarchy that runs from apprentice to line cook to sous-chef to chef de cuisine, the front of the house (or dining room) has a hierarchy of sorts. Barkeepers are assisted by barbacks, who might prep the juices for drinks or make some of the syrups for craft cocktails. During service they will replenish stemware, carry bussing trays full of dirty dishes to the back, or tap a keg that runs dry ("kicks" in barspeak). A main hostess might be aided by an assistant hostess who still hasn't mastered the technical aspects of reservation systems, but by walking the guests to the tables and depositing menus, she allows the main hostess to remain at the station, fielding calls and greeting customers at the door. Depending on the size of the operation, the restaurateur might be backed up by a general manager responsible for meeting guest-count projections and hiring staff, assistant general managers who are training to take on that role, and floor managers who might write schedules, program keys for new dishes on the order screen, and perhaps be given a single line—say laundry—of the profit-and-loss statement to oversee. Lien started out below this, a swing manager who spent her time between two restaurants. Not exactly the partner an overworked chef could toss projects to.

"He thought I was useless," Lien recalls of Jonathan. "It was like a new kid at school going in at midyear when everyone is looking at you. Where did you come from? He didn't think I had anything. It was very difficult to come into two new schools and to try and lead a restaurant into a night of success when your cohort in the kitchen thinks you're a joke." Hard as that stage was, Lien and Jonathan eventually came to understand they shared a mutual work ethic. That's shown by coming in early, staying late when necessary, not bailing at the first opportunity, and volunteering for shifts or events that take the requirements of the business into consideration. In restaurant parlance, it's called getting shit done. They each got shit done and, without realizing it at the time, took the first step toward their eventual partnership—and their success.

In the restaurant business it's not enough just to have a

great idea; it's not even enough to have a strategic plan and a great location, as necessary as both those things are. You've also got to wear lots of hats and multitask ad infinitum. You need to develop working relationships with city and state regulatory officials. You need to hire lawyers and woo investors to help behind the scenes. You need to join partners to either prepare the food or oversee the dining room. Assembling the best team possible is paramount to a successful launch.

ONE MORNING, OVER PANCAKES and refills of coffee at the Denny's near HLAY, Lien sits in a seat by the window recalling the love she'd developed for the food business while a student at Emerson College in Boston. She'd gone there to study magazine design and writing. One of her freshman friends, Katherine, took Lien to visit her family in New Orleans. "All the restaurants I'd gone to growing up were chain restaurants. I didn't really understand restaurants," she says and catches herself. "Waffle House, I understood."

Casting her mind back, she recalls a place that would prove crucial to her future. "New Orleans is actually how I attribute falling in love with real food. Katherine was born and bred in New Orleans, raised by a single mom. She said I would love it there and I should really consider coming home with her. So when I did go, turns out her mom was the wine director of chef-owner Susan Spicer's Bayona, and she lived in this tiny apartment in the Quarter. I ate around the city, I ate oysters and turtle soup for the first time in restaurants. I went back every summer. Her mom was an amazing cook. Best grits I've ever had."

For Lien, these summers were an awakening to the restaurant experience and the power of conviviality. The seed needed time to germinate, but now it had been planted. Soon after graduation she and her then boyfriend drove to Los Angeles, and after working briefly in a variety of stores, Lien started working at an entertainment website, providing material for one of its gossip columnists. It was 2004 and websites were just starting to find their place in an evolving media landscape. LA was a subject unto itself. "His column launched every Thursday. So I went to events and after-parties or a fragrance launch for Paris Hilton to interview celebrities, which was very hard for me, but I had to do it because it was my job. I had to get the attention of whatever celebrity. So if it was Hugh Jackman, I'd have to be, 'Hugh, I need you to get to me . . .' I'd go to all the awards shows. I'd roam around the Beverly Hilton and walk up to celebrities and ask the most ridiculous questions. I learned things about myself. I learned I could accomplish things instead of just being scared. I learned that other people cared about my job far more than I ever cared about my job because they were constantly asking me who was the favorite person I'd ever spoken to. I secretly felt ashamed because I wasn't having connected conversations with these people. Even at that young an age, that was what I cared most about, a connection with somebody."

In fact, between her daily tasks of reporting for this entertainment website and others—and often during them—she'd been hatching a plan to open a Vietnamese place that would somehow be both a small-plates restaurant and a cocktail bar. As a casual diner, she'd sensed the energy rush of being in a busy restaurant and was curious about how it must look from the other side—the inside. There were plates going out; there were happy people; there were all sorts of activities she didn't understand but that contributed to the atmosphere. Plus special restaurants always felt like they were giving voice to something more than food. In her case, this other dimension was a heritage that most times felt distant. Even though she'd grown up in the South, it was Vietnam that still provided a link to her past. She knew the name she wanted it to have, Bar Tet, and felt she knew the obvious entry point. "I thought I wanted to open a Vietnamese restaurant, something small, casual." Thinking back on it now, she sees it as an idea that was too obvious. "It's so stupid because there are so many. Why would I want to do the same thing?" That distinction is paramount in a successful restaurateur's skill set. Doing what has proven successful for others is not only too obvious but ultimately self-defeating. The public responds to a new formulation of what dining out looks like, and good restaurateurs provide it.

The dissatisfaction she'd been feeling at her job peaked in June 2009, when Michael Jackson and Farrah Fawcett died on the same day. "I think it was a combination of too many people dying and my job and I had just had it," Lien recalls. "I remember going home and thinking, this is not my life. I have to take action, what am I going to do? So I asked myself what makes me happy, and it was always food, a simple thing like a burger. I thought maybe I should open up a restaurant for real."

Nine months after quitting and taking some time off, she found a job as a brunch hostess at a newly launched tile-and-dark-wood spot on Sunset Boulevard in Hollywood. Brunch is famously unforgiving for restaurant workers. A room of impatient people with strollers is probably part of it. A mimosa doesn't take the edge off like a real drink. And the whole thing is built around eggs, an ingredient that *has* to be modified. Even so, Lien was able to make use of her time and learn a skill. "My first Sunday it was very busy, and what I observed was people at brunch can be very angry. There's usually a wait and all they want is coffee." Even under duress, a real sense of hospitality was soon coming through as she grew into her new role far from the red carpet. "I enjoyed speaking to people, giving them what they want. I just enjoyed looking at things from the other person's perspective. I get why you're upset. Do you want coffee? Let's get you seated."

She then started work as a floor manager at Picca, a modern Peruvian place in West LA that Lima-born chef Ricardo Zarate and restaurateur Stephane Bombet conceived. The music pounded, *yuzu kosho*–freighted dipping sauce was served alongside the *robata*-grilled skewers, and the dramatically shaken pisco sour cocktails were poured, weightless and frothy, in vintage wide-lipped glassware.

It was here that Lien started to acquire the skills that might lead to being a restaurateur. She learned to manage capital—she was in charge of daily opening, closing, and staffing—but also to navigate the requirements of human capital, how to keep the burned-out server engaged, for instance, or ensure service standards were being met by the team. As she adapted to the late-night restaurant life, she became aware of how much she enjoyed the challenges and the pressure. She stayed long after the party ended, when the coals in the *robata* were dying down, the AC had been turned off, the tips had been distributed, and the day's credit card transactions were closed out. And she loved it.

After she left her seventeen-month stint at Picca in December 2012, the speed with which she went from newly hired swing manager at Animal to a position created for her as "culinary liaison" says something about her organizational powers. She started as "Lien from Picca," but within a few months she was organizing Shook and Dotolo's travel schedules and media appearances, plus assisting during the construction stages of Jon & Vinny's, the duo's new casual pizzeria, all while grinding out mundane details of the business. Negotiating deals with waste management vendors? Call Lien. Her relationship with Jonathan was also progressing. He'd shown more interest in her opinion and appreciated the warmth she brought to any exchange. By mid-2013 she recognized a kindred spirit in him. By his own description a punk skater kid from Orange County, he, too, had fought for a sense of identity and found it in restaurants.

Soon after graduating from culinary school, Jonathan had left one restaurant because the wholesale produce trucks that arrived every morning didn't jive with the small-farmer-driven philosophy the restaurant professed. Under Per Se alum Matthew Accarrino at the newly opened Craft in Century City, he developed a fascination with the European tradition of artfully composed terrines and charcuterie programs. When he made it to Europe in 2010, he spent a few days *staging*, a short-term unpaid stint in a restaurant, in perhaps the last example of a fully funded, shiny white, brightly toqued kitchen brigade at Alain Ducasse's Le Louis XV at the Hôtel de Paris in Monte Carlo. It's an experience he still talks about almost with awe. "The sauce chef has tons of copper pots, all labeled with whatever they are for: There's venison, there's 'veal one'—it's like a lighter veal sauce—and there's 'veal two' for the heavier roasted meats," he recalls. "All this stuff got imprinted in my head. I'm a very visual person. I can just look at something and know what's going on. He takes all that—there's roasted chicken being picked up, the guy is carving the chicken and putting it on the platter, and he puts a little wet towel on it to keep it moist and then passes it down. The *entremetier* puts on the garnishes. By that point the bones have gone around to the sauce guy and he's smashing them down, sweating, hitting them with a reduction, and then straining it down to make the sauce perfect. It's like everything is . . .

It's just . . . The refortification of sauce making is what I learned in French cooking."

He also traveled to eat at the legendary Michel Bras's Le Suquet, a sleek modern structure in the French heartland. The trains had grown successively smaller to reach the village of Laguiole, but when he finally sat down at the white tablecloth, looked through the plate glass at the gorse and heather that stretched into the distance, and tasted the deeply rooted cooking, he knew the journey had been well worth it.

Jonathan then spent four months at Mirazur on the French Riviera. Located about two hundred yards from the Italian border in the scalloped inlet of Menton, the restaurant sat below a series of terraced gardens that provided the kitchen with produce. Every dawn the visiting *stagiaires*, those students and traveling cooks working for free, would wake up, pull on boots, and head up the hill with lists and baskets. What they picked would be on that night's menu— chef Mauro Colagreco thought up dishes that used whatever the young cooks brought him. It was an idyllic time for Jonathan. His height was handy when he'd hoist a smaller cook on his shoulders to pluck berries from otherwise unreachable ledges; the basic vocabulary he'd learned in strip mall sushi spots allowed him to serve as intermediary between the Japanese *chef de partie* and the local fishermen. Three *saba*? That was *trois maquereau*, three mackerel. Done. His work ethic was prized, too, and he would have returned for a second season, but a family medical emergency brought him home early, before the first season was even done.

Back in LA he landed a job under Tony Esnault at Patina, the restaurant adjacent to Frank Gehry's Walt Disney Concert Hall in downtown LA, and it was there that he perfected the slow-simmered, multistep art of sauce making—what he'd gotten a glimpse of at Le Louis XV—that would become a hallmark of his style. He moved to Mezze, an ambitious though failing Middle Eastern restaurant on La Cienega, in late 2012. When it shuttered, he sent out a group text to all his kitchen contacts. One answered immediately and sped him to Animal for a one-day tryout. In the kitchen they found Dotolo discussing with his cooks a recipe for beef heart. Jonathan recalled a recent meal with a friend in a small Russian restaurant on Santa Monica Boulevard that involved molded creamed herring and potatoes and dill, and volunteered a recipe of his own. He recalibrated it with pickled beets, paprika, and beef heart and to his amazement saw it printed on Animal's one-page menu soon thereafter. It wasn't long before Shook told him he was hired.

Jonathan would undoubtedly have become a chef without

those critical months in Europe, but such trips are a ritual for aspiring cooks who can save up the money required. Ostensibly they go to learn technique, but they also often return with greater confidence. Jonathan always encouraged the younger cooks at Animal to take *staging* trips. In fact it was at the going-away party for one of them that Lien first talked to him about Bar Tet.

"I think it was June of 2014 that I had the epiphany about Jonathan being the right chef," she says. "There was some guy who was leaving, he was going to do some *staging* in either Mexico City or Copenhagen, it was his last night as a cook and they were all going out that night for drinks to a strip club in Thai Town. I hadn't once gone out with the team and I was, 'I'd love to go out, I'll be there.' So we all go and I was stupidly excited all day and I wanted to find a good time to pitch my idea to Jonathan. And I'm drinking some whiskey. There's a pool table and I went around to where he was seated and I said, 'It doesn't have to be right now, but I have an idea I want to talk to you about.' He goes, 'OK,' and then I go sit somewhere else and he comes over and asks me what's the idea. He's a very fast-paced person, his mind works very quickly. He's very smart. I said, 'A long time ago when I first started working in restaurants the whole point was to open a Vietnamese concept where I'd do a bar, small bites, Vietnamese flavors but modern. And I thought you'd be a great chef for it.' He said, 'Sounds fun, sounds easy.' I felt very shy. I felt very exposed." She hadn't told her idea to many people, and Jonathan was certainly the first one who could actually make it happen.

Casual as the moment was, it marked a shift in their relationship from team members to potential partners. Jonathan drew up a menu of what the food might be like. It would be his take on Vietnam, nothing to do with Europe or Animal. Still, neither thought they had much more than a concept and a sketched-out selection of dishes. Hardly enough to bank their future on. The responsibilities of running one of the hottest restaurants in the country left Jonathan with little time to think about the project much further, but Lien, determined to open something, would eventually leave Animal in September 2014 so she could concentrate on it. She didn't want her research to be done while on another restaurateur's payroll, and she needed time to sort through the ideas she had. Bar Tet was certainly one. But so was a short-lived idea to partner with a friend on a dumpling takeaway spot on Los Angeles's Westside. There were days when her head teemed with possibilities until finding a location finally honed them into one.

To a potential restaurateur, the city is full of leads for

a possible location. The ground floor of every new condo building beckons. Contractors have their ears to the ground. Brokers can be an invaluable resource. But so are storefront signs. Even extended happy hours are signals. You shouldn't need to offer $5 Jameson shots on a Friday night if you're making money. Lien found the location that would become HLAY through an acquaintance of her then fiancé, Julian Fang, an early member of the team at Wolvesmouth, a pop-up that had been written about in the *New Yorker*. Fang knew Jimmy Han, a real estate investor and craft beer connoisseur who created Beer Belly, a beer hall in a lot on Western between 5th and 6th Streets. In a short time, Jimmy had doubled down on the neighborhood. He had launched a Philly cheesesteak sandwich place named Whiz at the corner of 6th and Oxford, but for a number of reasons it was not doing well. At a February 2015 dinner, Han mentioned he was looking for someone to take it over. Lien contacted him within days.

Lien knew that even though Jimmy was an acquaintance, this was business and she would be sized up like every potential tenant. "He's a landlord and sees people all the time," she says. "But do they have capital? Can they sign a lease at the end of the month and drop fifteen Gs?" Even without anything close to the amount it would take to open a restaurant in the corner space on 6th Street, she got to see it. In addition to the sandwich shop, small adjoining businesses had all left marks of their passage behind. The psychic had left the sign, the nail salon a foot bath. Lien knew it was too large to house a concept as cozy as Bar Tet. It was Jonathan when he visited who immediately sensed the potential that the location held to be a chef-driven restaurant in the heart of Koreatown.

Working out of her one-bedroom Venice apartment, Lien now set about crafting a business plan that drew on all her writing skills. She gave lyrical descriptions of the neighborhood and compressed information into bullet points that would be easily understandable to potential investors. She and Jonathan wanted these investors to put in a total of $850,000, which then became $750,000. They slowly accumulated sums ranging from $25,000 to $200,000 from all sorts of people who believed in them, usually after they ate Jonathan's food. Often, chefs cook for potential investors in their homes to raise funds, since it is more casual than going to the restaurant and there's more opportunity to talk. With an already crazy schedule, this was an additional task for Jonathan, but sitting down with investors between courses was a good way to explain the project. Cooking these dinners was also a way of fine-tuning their ideas for the menu.

For one salad, he bought loaves of dark rye bread from one of the old Russian bakeries in West Hollywood. He cubed the bread and roasted it slowly with cultured butter and garlic. Then he dried the cubes and ran them through a sieve. He scattered the earthy, molasses-tinged bread crumbs over a whipped Syrian feta with sweet but firm nectarines and handfuls of purslane. It was, he believes, what inspired TV producer and food personality Phil Rosenthal to sign on as an investor. Those moments were windfalls that helped Lien's idea become more than a bootstrapped dream and for the restaurant to slowly become a reality.

They're long since scattered, but the notebooks and scratch paper Lien maintained between August 2015, when they took over the space, and July 2016, when they opened, would have contained an impressive number of crossed-out lists. On top of continuing to raise funds, Lien was working her way through the requirements the city demanded. She prayed for the Los Angeles Department of Water and Power to finally turn on the meter, she tracked down the one person in the Department of Building and Safety who could issue the certificate of occupancy, and she and Jonathan white-knuckled the visit from the Los Angeles County Department of Public Health. Between those junctures they designed the interior. "Suddenly I would have three days to figure out Title 24–compliant lights," Lien recalls. Their plans to serve full liquor involved obtaining a change-of-use permit, a process that took up much of her time. She had to attend an interview with LAPD Vice Division detectives. They made her promise she wouldn't be serving shots at 2 a.m. They told her to lose the front patio she envisioned but allowed her to move the process on to the next stage: sending one thousand notices of their liquor-sales application to everyone who lived within five hundred feet (and nursing paper cuts). With that done, she paid $58,000 for one of two liquor licenses her broker found being offered in Los Angeles (they are notoriously hard to win) and signed personal guarantees to all the liquor distributors who insisted on it before delivering a single case. Succeed or fail, she was on the hook for it all.

As the opening approached, Lien had to figure out the landing page for the website and choose an Instagram handle. She hired her first front-of-house staff. Kelly, a hostess, came through a friend of a friend who knew someone at Jon & Vinny's. Mark, a server with a great résumé, was referred. Drew, an actor from San Francisco, answered an ad on Craigslist. "GREAT WAITER" read the subject line of his reply. And when he showed up in a cutoff denim-washed vest, both Lien and Jonathan liked his energy and hired him, too. But hiring a tentative staff was only one line on her list. She had to order more fish sauce, bandages, plates, and those energy-saving Title 24–compliant light bulbs. It seemed the lists would never end, until they did. On July 13, 2016, they opened Here's Looking at You. Kelly barely had time to construct the IKEA piece they'd bought to serve as a hostess stand as Lien gathered herself to lead the preshift meeting. Drew was there. So was Mark. Lien tried to keep the discussion to practical information about the ingredients of cocktails and dishes, but the months of work had taken a toll. "Lien grew really emotional," Jonathan recalls. "'I can't talk anymore,' she said. 'I just need to go. Let's open.'" And with that they rolled up the metal shutters on the restaurant's door.

3

OPERATOR

For the first few months after they opened, Jonathan was so short-staffed that a cook friend who'd worked with him before came in at six every evening to work the expediting pass. At that metal table by the kitchen door—watched over by a photograph of Lemmy, the bass guitarist from Motörhead, on stage—those early dishes produced by HLAY's kitchen were inspected and wiped clear of smudges or fingerprints before being sent out into the dining room. Much has changed since then. When Jonathan posts a job opening online, he receives hundreds of replies from across the country. No longer "Lien from Picca," Lien is often asked to be a guest speaker; her opinion is sought out, and she has earned the right to be called a restaurateur. It's not a term she would have dreamt of when her résumé amounted to being a good writer, interviewer, and eater who could host a brunch shift. It is one that she shies from using even today. "My job is to pay back my investors," Lien will say, matter-of-factly. In a more introspective moment, she'll admit, "I don't know, I needed purpose, I needed to flex whatever skills I had."

"Restaurant operator" could be considered a more practical term. There are enough moving parts to suggest something mechanical about running a restaurant. But that can also seem to steal some of the romance of going out to eat. A restaurant is, after all, that place someone heads to for the farmstead cheeseboard, or to eat A5 Wagyu beef for the first time, or simply for the pleasure of sipping a well-made old-fashioned in a crystal double-rocks glass. Even those who don't know the details of each role and piece of the puzzle are aware when some part is missing, just as they can also sense when the lyrical matches the practical, hospitality warms execution, and the puzzle is whole. Only "restaurateur" can really capture all that.

Still, Lien's hesitation to use the term is understandable. She was, after all, originally aiming to create a cozy, Vietnamese-slanted small-plate, cocktail-driven venture, and the grand associations with the word "restaurateur" seem wildly out of scale with what she was trying to achieve. But just as the role of restaurateur has evolved throughout history, so have the people who can become one. Minorities and women are among the groups who have helped redefine a profession that requires both a sense of hospitality and enough financial smarts to make a venture succeed. Instead of being an archaic term, it is one that reflects its times.

Admittedly it took some doing. Unlike so many other titles in the restaurant business that seem to contain all the irreverent delight of American English—"fry cook," "barfly," "soda jerk," and "hash slinger" come to mind—there's no cheeky term for the person who runs a restaurant. The designation "restaurateur" dates to the years after the French Revolution when the cooks of the nobility left their posts to serve the working classes. Having eaten, the customer would in a certain way feel *restored*. Through the eighteenth century, American dining had the opposite effect. It was irrepressibly vital. This was a country of taverns and saloons, beaneries, luncheonettes, and chophouses. The food was fast, the bill of fare was in cents, speed was paramount, refills were free. Customers were not "restored"; they were fed. The person for whom the restaurant might be named had enough self-importance to send someone else out to the pavement to promote what the kitchen offered. "At Sweeney's we save our sixpence and dispense with superfluities," wrote George G. Foster in a nicely turned restaurant roundup appearing in the *New York Tribune* of the late 1840s.

By the end of the nineteenth century, a new type of proprietor starts appearing in sepia photographs. Mustachioed men, thumbs in their watch pockets, their best bowler hats sitting atop their heads, these restaurant owners stand alongside their apron-wearing crews, newsboys, brewery cart drivers, and anyone else who happened to be at the establishment when the photographer stopped by. These dining establishments still had the soul of saloons, but something was beginning to change. At places like Delmonico's and Sherry's, which catered to the upper echelons of New York City society, owners reigned over the dining rooms. Unlike Sweeney's and its ilk, these establishments were overseen by individuals who cultivated the conditions—the setting, the wine list, the worthy destination—that made potential customers eager to book a table. These were the first American restaurateurs.

By the 1940s, yet another more professional class of restaurateurs appeared. Some in the business had thrived during Prohibition; others came onto the scene during the post–World War II boom years. Establishments such as Toots Shor's, Dinty Moore's, Chasen's, and Jack and Charlie's (a predecessor of New York's 21 Club) expanded the definition of the restaurant. The men who ran these establishments acted as businessmen with decidedly public personas.

A regular business owner might be known to his employees, but only a restaurateur had to be known, and perhaps even adored, by his potential customers. Typical of such men was Milwaukee's Karl Ratzsch, who ran an exposed-beam Mason Street establishment (naturally named Karl Ratzsch). A local newspaper had described the tavern keeper who put young Ratzsch into business as "a typical Mein Host," but the dark-suited Ratzsch, at the door and ready to welcome regulars, was the embodiment of a restaurateur.

Ratzsch shuttered in 2017 (not before this reporter got to sample their sauerbraten with gingersnap gravy at the worn wood counter). But the mode of restaurateur he made famous was challenged long before then. The contest occurred in New York in the 1950s. Henri Soulé, the celebrated owner of Le Pavillon, who had come to the US aboard the *Normandie* to represent French gastronomy at the 1939 World's Fair, was a restaurateur in Ratzsch's image. At Le Pavillon, the gilded and exclusive establishment across from the St. Regis hotel on 55th Street, Soulé stood guard at the door. Brilliant, jowly, snobbish, "a martinet" in the words of longtime *New York* magazine restaurant critic Gael Greene, Soulé was enough of a character to warrant a *New Yorker* profile. It's the words of Joseph Wechsberg that bring the five-foot-five Basque legend back to life: "It is almost impossible to dine at the Pavillon without encountering Soulé. He tries to greet each guest at the door and to say goodbye to each later. He pilots the customers to their tables or, if he can't take the time for that, instructs one of his captains to do so, and he also pilots them past the unmapped shallows and reefs of the menu, suggesting plats du jour and recommending wines. During a lull, he is likely to serve a customer himself—carving a *carré de chevreuil flambé* at a table. The rest of the time, he is rushing to answer the telephone, whispering orders to his subordinates, initialing the checks of customers whose credit is good, or placing a centerpiece just so."

Three blocks away at the Four Seasons, the high-ceilinged Philip Johnson–designed architectural temple occupying the ground floor of the Seagram Building on 52nd Street, Joe Baum, the genius behind Restaurant Associates, a company that grew out of the Riker's coffee shop chain, chose a different path, one that didn't require initialing chits but that was no less special. With a flaming wall of chickens (La Fonda del Sol), bartenders in leather jerkins (Forum of the Twelve Caesars), and plenty of cool modernism (the Four Seasons), RA properties were attractions that depended on no one individual to attract guests.

In hindsight, what was being settled was the role of restaurateur. The success Soulé had known was predicated on his presence. During the summer months, he closed his Manhattan restaurant, loaded a van with pots, cooks, and waiters, and moved his whole operation to East Hampton to cater to his clientele at the Hedges Inn, that much closer to their seaside estates. Baum understood that the *team* of people welcoming, cooking, and serving was the show. The restaurateur still had to have vision. And he had to facilitate. But he didn't necessarily have to stand at the door.

That insight has become increasingly important as restaurants have shifted from single business to multiunit restaurant groups. Every city has one or more versions, loosely following the game plan of Richard Melman of Chicago's Lettuce Entertain You Enterprises, which already in 1971 found operating a diversity of restaurant types more rewarding than fast food's single-concept, multistate approach. Tom Douglas's collection of taverns, diners, pizzerias, and grill rooms fills the role in Seattle. The businesses that have grown out of the Highlands Bar & Grill in Birmingham, Alabama, offer folks a variety of ways to enjoy chef Frank Stitt's cooking. Drew Nieporent, a graduate of the Cornell School of Hotel Administration, one of the premier programs in the country, operates individual landmarks such as Tribeca Grill, Bâtard, and the Manhattan location of Nobu. For each of these individuals there are benefits of operating several restaurants. These might be the lower prices they can negotiate because of their combined purchasing power, the ability to recruit from a homegrown pool of talent, or the messaging focus of having an in-house PR representative. It's also a scale that allows them to interact with real estate concerns that need them as tenants to burnish high-priced developments. A popular restaurant on the ground floor enhances a gleaming condo tower in a way that a Duane Reade drugstore does not.

If RESTAURATEUR IS NO longer a profession that requires one's presence at the restaurant, it demands, as it always has, great financial insight at every step of the way. Which may be why a restaurant-management class at Los Angeles Trade-Tech College on the southwest edge of downtown LA is already full of eager students on a winter morning when restaurateur Donato Poto walks in. Poto, a lively fifty-four-year-old from southern Italy, embodies old-world charm. Together with chef Michael Cimarusti he operates Providence, LA's premier seafood destination; Connie and Ted's, an homage to Italian-American seafood dining;

and Il Pesce Cucina, a third concept, this one built around grilled seafood, in the recently opened Eataly complex that occupies a massive extension of the Westfield Century City Mall on LA's Westside. A few of the students are sent to greet Donato at the parking structure, and wearing a lavender V-neck cashmere sweater, he smiles in the relaxed way restaurateurs do when—for once—they don't have to take care of all the details. All he has to do is talk.

It's not long before the subject turns to leases. "How do you go about getting a location?" asks a young woman in a hoodie from the third row.

Had he been at the door of Providence, where he switches between four languages with a cosmopolitan ease, he might have given a sunnier answer. But these twenty-four culinary students had signed up for this additional class that is strategically scheduled for a Friday so all can attend. They had come by bus and train, some from many miles away. They had spoken earlier of starting food trucks and little places that reflected their varied heritages. Clearly, Poto felt he owed them an honest answer.

"When you buy a restaurant, you buy the business, which is nothing," he said. "If the place is bankrupt, the landlord is desperately looking for you. You just pay the rent."

Given the stakes, restaurateurs think long and hard before committing to a lease and a location. Big questions swirl around the decision: Is there foot traffic? Can I generate enough sales to pay for this? Taking on the responsibility of a lease still gives pause to a restaurateur as experienced as Danny Meyer, the founder of the New York–based Union Square Hospitality Group. "Even today, I still ask for a transferable lease," he writes in his memoir, *Setting the Table*. In 1985 he approached the notion of taking over a decades-old vegetarian restaurant that would be his first restaurant with enormous apprehension. Union Square Café, a warm three-level room with a balcony and modern art, would eventually become a destination. It also made it possible for Union Square Park to regain its role as the vital public space it had been before it became a sketchy area best avoided.

Like Manhattan, Los Angeles is a city constantly expanding possible locations for ambitious restaurants—and turning real estate equations on their head. To restaurateurs, who read the shifting urban landscape with different criteria than most other businesspeople, a turnkey location in Beverly Hills or Santa Monica becomes less appealing than a warehouse with the possibility of a patio set amid body shops bordering the LA river on the city's east side. *That* is not obvious. It was with that sense of the potential of the city that in 2016, the same year Lien and Jonathan opened

HLAY, and not that far away, chef Kevin Meehan and his front-of-the-house business partner Drew Langley found a brick row building in an undeveloped neighborhood enticingly close to Paramount Pictures' main gate.

"We kicked tires for three years," Langley recalled of those early days searching for a location. Previous to owning Kali, a market-driven neighborhood favorite where pale walls are brightened with sound-dampening turquoise fabric panels, Langley worked as a wine salesman at Greenblatt's deli on Sunset Boulevard, as a sommelier at fussy (and now defunct) places like L'Orangerie, and even as a cellar rat at a high rollers' wine-storage facility in Beverly Hills. He moves with the dexterity of someone used to handling heavy cases in tight spaces. "And it really ended up coming down to a real estate deal. We knew how to manage a restaurant from our different aspects, but we needed to find a place that had that Goldilocks thing with the right rent, the parking, the right conditional use permit, the licensing, and the lease. It was a combination of things that made sense."

He and Meehan learned to stake places out. They would go at seven, and then they would circle back after their separate shifts. "We just went," he says. "Even if it was a shithole, it was an exercise." By seeing every location, they learned to ask questions about everything from bar plumbing to disability bathroom access to cranky neighbors. Most importantly, they learned to read the liquor licenses. "You can have a liquor license, and it will say 'for this address,' and it will actually have the whole building. It will be different places that share a license. We looked at this place in Silver Lake, and that was the case entirely. We were hot for it, we wanted it, it was a big restaurant and we were going to do catering stuff out of the back," he explained. "And then we found out that the liquor license is shared with the bar next door, which is this hipster place, which is cute and I dig it, but . . . I don't know what they're doing, I don't know how they operate. I don't know who's in charge over there and I can't . . . *risk* it."

By "it" he means their investors' money. Like Lien and Jonathan had done, Meehan and Langley were trying to raise money as they were looking for a location. They, too, had a magic number. Much of the $650,000 Langley and Meehan raised—a full $100,000 short of what they'd hoped for—was from people close to them. It still surprised Langley. "All these people that were whispering in our ear for years and years, 'Hey, when you guys do your own thing, let me know, I want to get in on it.' A lot of those people didn't come to the table when it came to it. And we were really surprised by the people that did give us money. It was like friends and neighbors, an electrician from Paramount with a kid, people who knew us and believed in us, which is very humbling but it's also motivational, too."

The subscription agreement they drew up with investors is a fairly standard one; Langley and Meehan each own 30 percent of the restaurant, and the other 40 percent is divided among their nineteen investors. Kali operates profitably, but until the entire capital has been repaid, Meehan and Langley receive only a set salary and can't participate in the profit sharing. That day seems inevitable. In their first year they were able to return 27 percent of the investment to their backers. In order to do so, they started their work as soon as possible.

"Once the lease is in your name, you have to reopen in order to keep your conditional use permit," Langley says. "That's how things are grandfathered in. You don't close for a number of months because then you have to go back in and retrofit and be reinspected by the city. And so you have to flip it in a very short period of time and you can't do any major renovation. The only thing we really did was clean the hell out of the place and we took out the booths. There was a glass wall with a weird encased smoking area, we took that out and it opened the whole thing." Because of the shortfall in the budget, there were concessions. Meehan got some secondhand heat lamps that he painted blue—but not the walk-in fridge he wanted. Instead of a dedicated room Langley made do with a couple of temp-controlled wine coolers to keep his wines. "It was just Kevin and myself and a contractor and his assistant, and we did it all ourselves. We had to get open because we didn't have capital. We just needed to start generating money as quickly as possible. Especially when we hired people."

THOSE EARLY HIRES FOR Lien and Jonathan were crucial to establishing HLAY's philosophy. Some prospects with great résumés quickly flamed out—one after a single shift. When hiring, Lien is looking for far more than credentials. She wants candidates to be able to sound enthusiastic. "They have to convince me at the time of the interview that they can sell," she says. Sometimes she'll ask them to describe a favorite dish from a past restaurant or the favorite thing their mom made. "You have to sell it to me," she says. When Kelly dropped around the first time, the restaurant wasn't yet open. Lien and Kelly, then twenty years old, sat at the bar counter with carpenter's trestles about them. They spoke about clothing and music and what the restaurant that was taking shape around them would be like. It's a bond that occasionally appears in the brevity and naturalness of their exchanges. "Hey girl," Lien texted Kelly one morning, "just a heads up none of the resos have been confirmed." The tight bond that can form between restaurateur and employee notwithstanding, labor is one of the largest expenses in any restaurant's budget.

With contingencies for flow-through profit, above- and below-the-line expenses, and period projections, budgets can seem impossibly dense to anyone without a degree in accounting. But there are some simple concepts to remember. For example, when discussing the economics of a restaurant, it is useful to think of two meters running side by side, as the electricity and water might in a building. One meter is counting expenses; the other is counting revenue. It goes without saying that if the business is to stay solvent, the revenue meter must always be registering larger numbers. But they are not independent of each other. The numbers on the expense meter are required to produce the numbers on the revenue meter. And so, while direct expenses such as laundry, cutlery purchases, and flower arrangements play an important role in a restaurant's financial health, they are not nearly as critical as prime costs, which represent two-thirds of a restaurant's expenses in the form of labor and food cost.

That applies to the mom-and-pop place you go to for udon noodles and to the checkered tablecloth one with the wicker-wrapped Chianti bottles hanging from the rafters, and to the venue that morphs into a nightclub with an infinity pool. To even take a cursory look over American restaurant statistics is to a see a massive $799 billion industry that employs 10 percent of the workforce. One study puts a first-year failure rate at 26 percent, which highlights the importance of controlling the numbers.

There's a simple enough formula to determine labor cost: divide labor dollars by revenue, and multiply by one hundred. For example, if the front-of-the-house labor for one dinner service was $1,000 and revenue was $10,000, then the labor cost is 10 percent. Not great if it's an average cost to staff a dining room with servers, bussers, and a bar team (most restaurants aim for around 8 percent average) but not bad, either. Those interconnected numbers are a good way to look at the success of any food service operation. The five assistants in a totally empty new organic ice cream store are frantically waving at you to come in because the labor meter is whirling like a banshee's spindle while the revenue one isn't moving at all. And they know it. On the other hand, that ill-fated brunch where coffee finally arrived after you finished your waffle will have great labor numbers but at the price of guest satisfaction. If, instead of labor cost, the success of the food service operation was measured in the likelihood of return visits, the number wouldn't be great at all. Every restaurant has to balance labor cost against revenue and guest satisfaction. Which is why staffing is a complex issue. Cutting staff—running lean, as Lien and Jonathan did when HLAY opened—is not necessarily a long-term solution. The promptness with which sufficient cooks on the kitchen line can get orders out makes a good impression on a first-time guest. Extra servers on the floor have time to refresh drinks, talk up nightly specials, and provide the detailed service that also encourages return visits. In other words, a restaurant can push the revenue meter significantly ahead of the labor-cost one if everything is working as it should.

Such procedures are all part of a larger business plan that Lien wrote before the restaurant even opened, when she was sitting in her Venice one-bedroom. "You have to imagine what your dining room is going to look like," she says. "What's the capacity, how many people will it take to work that kind of service?" These business projections represent hard numbers for investors but also an important step in determining how a venture will operate. "So if you're going to project that every single person who comes to the restaurant is going to spend $60 per person, you break it down: $40 of this will be for food, $20 will be liquor. Eighty-five people will come on a Monday, 125 will come on a Saturday."

Luckily she's not in the math game alone; a chef is as responsible as the person running the dining room for ensuring profitable numbers. Like labor, food cost is a matter of balance: in this case, the price of the ingredients plus the labor it costs to transform them into a final dish divided by the price it is sold for. Say it costs $2 to make those glistening chicken wings with a spicy glaze shouting out at you from a gastropub's menu. Divided by the $10.99 they are offered at, the food cost clocks in at 18 percent. It's tricky, in fact impossible, to get that kind of low percentage when the price of the ingredients is already high. And so, though it's not quite an algorithm, there're an awful lot of counterbalancing forces that go into the final equation—and a restaurateur is constantly adjusting.

For Lien, the margins on liquor present one way to offset a bump in food cost. "Liquor will always be key for us. It saves us in many ways," she says. "We're good at it and we provide great quality." The wine list, which Lien and wine director Danielle Françoise Fournier put together, is also extremely affordable (most wines are under $100) and creates an opportunity to bring awareness to unsung grape types. "We might price a California chardonnay a little higher if we

believe guests are ordering it simply because they're familiar with Cali chardonnay," Lien says. "Then we might price
some lesser-known grape a little lower, to bring awareness to
something we love that would go great with Jonathan's food."

Jonathan similarly tweaks the cost of the dishes he puts
on the menu, coming in low on one creation, giving him the
room to go higher in another. One morning, in the quiet of
HLAY's empty dining room, Jonathan busies himself with
paperwork at a table. Last night was a long one, and he is
moving slowly, deliberately, the way chefs do early in the
day. HLAY's one-page menu lies on the table before him.
It's a compressed twenty-to-thirty-item list: shishito peppers amped with *huamei*, a Chinese salted plum powder, and
heirloom tomato wedges freighted with earthy rendered
Vietnamese *lap xuong* sausage, all of which sound enticing
to a customer but to him form a series of related parts.

He is keeping track of the cost. The arithmetic is not so
complicated that he can't perform it on his phone's calcula-
tor to get the results. "Let's do a play on beef cheeks and
slow braise them in dashi," he says as he punches some numbers in to the screen. "Beef cheeks are expensive, $8 or $9
a pound when you cut down to the meat. I want to charge
only so much because the portion is small, but I'll make it up
on another dish. The garnishes aren't that much. Call it $2

just to be safe. If my sous-chef does the butchering, he's one of my highest-paid guys, so I have to figure it's an hour of his time. We're not going to go down to $6.98. I'll round it out to $7. That's per portion. Most restaurants get a case of beef cheeks and they'll price how much it costs to cook them all. I may only need ten portions, so I'd rather do it by the portion." The menu price is $26. He cocks an eyebrow because he's up at 27 percent food cost—above where he'd like to be. But pork shanks aren't expensive, and when he renders them slowly in fat, shreds and serves them as carnitas with a forceful kimchi verde, the food cost percentage is still a reasonable 12 percent. Low enough to allow him to run the beef cheeks at a profitable price. Lien would approve.

She performs a similar arithmetic for wine. It follows pretty much the same formula—except with the additional complication that many customers now look up the bottle price on their phone before ordering. It's as if before choosing the beef cheeks, they checked the wholesale cost on a meat-price app. It's no secret that the restaurant industry prices wine by the glass for what it costs them to purchase it by the bottle. Depending on what side of the counter you're on, that can either be described as 25 percent cost (by the restaurateur) or a 400 percent markup (by the customer). There is profit there, of course, but the restaurateur also takes into account paying for glassware, a person to pour it (and ideally refill it), and another person to wash and perhaps even stock the wine room, all in a venue that's fully paid up with permits and licenses.

But the most important equation, the one that serves as a cornerstone to a restaurant's financials, is COGS, or cost of goods sold. Even in an industry that delights in Pentagon-ish acronyms—renting out the back room for parties is part of your MRS (multiple revenue stream) strategy—COGS felicitously sound like exactly what they do: drive the financial mechanism.

The equation: Beginning inventory plus purchases minus ending inventory equals COGS. With that, a bigger picture than day-to-day operation becomes apparent—one that allows a restaurateur to see the difference between a good night and a good month. When COGS is divided by food sales for a period, the result is the food, liquor, wine, and beer cost for the entire period. And when that number is subtracted from total sales, you get gross profit. You still haven't subtracted operating costs like rent and labor, or annoying ones like the repeated visits the plumber made to fix the water heater, but you're well on your way to establishing net profit.

Inventory is central to this process. And any restaurant that wants to stay in business takes it seriously. So it's no surprise to find out that at the three restaurants chef David LeFevre, a former head sous-chef under legendary Chicago chef Charlie Trotter, who moved West in the early aughts, runs in the coastal town of Manhattan Beach, inventory is constantly assessed. His restaurants are all within three blocks of each other and a block from the beach. On the morning of the last day of the period, when a light sea mist envelops each restaurant, the crew of managers and supervisors are at work. In the attic above M.B. Post, a small-plates restaurant with a global cuisine, manager Brendan is crouching under beams, counting cases of Central Coast pinots. Two doors away, at Fishing with Dynamite, a New England clam-shack-type place with a busy oyster bar, chef Alex is counting the bushels of Kusshis and pristine New Zealand Coromandels they serve at the small bar.

Down the street at the Arthur J, a midcentury steak house built around a wood-burning grill from legendary Mesquite, Texas, grill manufacturer J&R, the team is also in inventory mode. General manager Alex was up until one in the morning counting bottles in the wine room, and manager Lily is taking stock of small-batch rye and bourbon at the bar. Downstairs in the prep kitchen, pastry cooks Matt and Marisol are eyeballing flour left in bins.

Though chef LeFevre's shaggy beard and Persol sunglasses give him the appearance of a California native, he was born in the Midwest. He was in his fourth year of engineering school at the University of Wisconsin in Madison when he decided to become a chef. The level of math he'd acquired by then allows him to explain the importance of inventory in simple terms. "I'm going to dumb it down a little," he says, easing into one of the Arthur J's booths. "You have two cartons of milk in the refrigerator. You buy two more cartons. And you end up with zero cartons of milk. How much did we use? Four. Our cost was four gallons, our purchases was two. If I counted just our purchases, it would have been two gallons of milk, but if I do inventory and I notice, oh, we have two less than we had at the beginning, it's 100 percent more. So our cost is four gallons versus two. So costs and purchases are very different. You can purchase stuff, but if you also use stuff that's on the shelf, your cost increases."

He then puts it into real terms. "So I start with $100,000 of wine, and I purchase $40,000. So I should have $140,000 that I started with and that I purchased. Now if I end up with $90,000 at the end of the month, I used $10,000 that we had sitting on the shelf, plus the $40,000, now it's $50,000. It's not just what you bought; it's what you're using that you already had sitting there. Your cost is 25 percent more than you might be thinking it is. And that's why places close.

Because they don't know. They don't know what their cost actually is."

A WORKING RESTAURANT CAN at times seem like a numbers game, some complicated piece of accounting whose final result is a well-executed meal. But having a solid financial framework is what allows a business to engage with society at a deeper level, to be in a position to demonstrate what's important to them. Financial stability allows the luxury of tackling other challenges; when you're not worrying how to stay afloat, you can work to solve greater issues. One that has been on Lien's mind recently is her role as a female restaurateur—a group that once counted few other than Ella Brennan. It's a subject that's important to her but one she also shies from making categorical statements about. Lien wasn't able to get a woman backer for HLAY—though, with a characteristic pivot to the positive, she notes that she has great, supportive male backers, not to mention Jonathan, her partner in the business.

Lien believes it's a topic that must be discussed in the industry, and she participates in panels with contemporaries in Los Angeles, and formidable pioneers such as Nancy Silverton, who launched La Brea Bakery and Campanile with Mark

Peel in 1989, and Mary Sue Milliken, who together with Susan Feniger was among the city's first female restaurateurs.

They launched City Café on Melrose Avenue in 1981, but their journey began when Milliken and Feniger met in the kitchen of Chicago's Le Perroquet in the late 1970s. There, the Midwest effort they put in (Milliken is from Michigan, Feniger from Ohio) brought them to the attention of the owner Jovan Trboyevic. The polished Yugoslav, who operated Le Perroquet in a Chicago town house, had connections throughout the food world. He got Milliken into the same kind of hardscrabble French kitchen that later helped Jonathan reach the next step in his career, Restaurant D'Olympe in Paris. Separately, Feniger had been able to intern at the prestigious Michelin-starred restaurant L'Oasis in the South of France. At the end of their training, they reconvened at Milliken's garret near the Vaugirard metro station. Over bottles of red wine, the two friends planned their next step. "We felt we were done learning," Milliken recently recalled. "We were done working under the man. The only way to get ahead was to be your own boss."

After Europe, Milliken returned to Chicago. Feniger headed to LA, and it was only a few months before the city's innovative fine dining scene brought them back together as partners. Certainly there was the clubby Continental sphere of dining that any American city could have produced at the time, but there were also restaurants doing things in a fresh way. Michael McCarty, one of the pioneers of California cuisine, had already opened Michael's in a former pub in Santa Monica. Restaurants such as L'Ermitage provided service on a cavalcade of Christofle dining room carts while also offering a soulful, produce-driven version of French gastronomy—chef Jean Bertranou even raised moulard ducks! At small places like Bruce Marder's West Beach Café in Venice, the chef melded the flavors he'd picked up in North Africa with the technique he'd learned under German chefs at the Beverly Hills Hotel. Ken Frank's La Toque, located at the foot of the Chateau Marmont's driveway, went one step further by taking for its name the very symbol of professional gastronomy: the tall white hat worn by classically trained chefs. Sure, it wasn't hard to goose its ambitions: La Toque was an easy pun away from La Toke, and the classic phrase at the top of the menu, *"La brigade de Ken Frank vous propose,"* proved irresistible to sharp-eyed critics. It was, wrote Colman Andrews in the pages of *New West*, "a phrase which doubtless gives pause to at least some of La Toque's customers, who are likely to think that a brigade is something that puts out fires and not something that poaches eels and broils ducks."

The restaurant did, however, engage with its customers in a way that others—with their air of reserve—did not. Frank hit up strip mall markets for ingredients such as ginger, soy, and even fresh basil. In the dining room, a group of budding gastronomes might be enjoying the *saumon en papillote* a table away from the retired Bette Davis, who, on hot nights, crossed Sunset Boulevard from her high-ceilinged apartment on Havenhurst Avenue to enjoy the restaurant's AC.

Feniger and Milliken took over a café in 1981. It had previously been a struggling espresso bar operated by the owners of l.a. Eyeworks. They agreed to transfer operations to Feniger and Milliken. What the two chefs cooked in their early menus wasn't stylistically groundbreaking, but their approach was, both in terms of the kitchen and the front of house. The rustic sensibility behind, say, a duck confit dish represented a point of view, one that would allow them to introduce other cuisines such as Indian, Mexican, and Thai. What's more, they were bosses now. These two women who in early coverage smile out from under their spiky '80s haircuts (they traded lunch for them with a nearby hairdresser) represented the growing ranks of women restaurateurs. Lidia Bastianich would open Felidia in Manhattan in 1981. With Chez Panisse's Alice Waters as a model in the Bay Area, Joyce Goldstein opened Square One in 1984, and the inimitable Barbara Tropp launched China Moon Cafe in San Francisco in 1986.

These women set the stage for Lien and other women restaurateurs some thirty years later. And though she's aware of and grateful for the expansion of opportunities other generations made possible, she's had to learn on her own how to be a boss. It didn't happen quickly. She learned tricks. She copes with the constant pressure of being a businesswoman with steady attendance at yoga classes and acupuncture sessions— okay, *and* an occasional phone call to a psychic. When faced with a tense situation, she slows her speech, which works a lot better than raising her voice. The skill that is hardest for her is delegating. "I don't know how to fully let go," she says with a laugh. She is learning to be adept at *not* doing it herself. It takes patience to not answer the important email she sees come in at 8 a.m. and instead allow a new manager to reply at 1 p.m. when they arrive for their shift. The challenge to erase herself is as real to her today as learning any of the other skills she has in her journey. "How do I make my team members be less dependent on me?" she asks. "How do I empower them so they believe what they do is better than what I would have done?" It's the question of a real restaurateur.

4

LEADER

It's a Friday night at HLAY and the operation is humming. That means that the tables are crowded; the clamor of conversation rises above the steady bass line of the music. After topping off a table with a Sierra Foothills chenin blanc and punching two new tiki-inspired cocktails into the POS, Drew, the actor from San Francisco, moves toward a two-top that's just been seated. In the kitchen, sous-chef Ken fires order after order of fried-octopus hush puppies, set gem-like into a circle of crème fraîche–boosted Kewpie mayonnaise. Bracing in its use of everyday ingredients—and at $12, affordable—the dish is selling so much it keeps the cook who has to construct each order a blur until the kitchen slows at 11 p.m.

By midnight the lights are up, the music is off, the bar team has wiped the counter and placed caps over the liquor bottles to prevent fruit flies. Lien is in the office calculating tips. Lien believes in pooled rather than individual tips, where servers pay out a determined percentage to other members of the front-of-house staff. At HLAY, the amount is determined by a points system, predetermined fractions of the total tip amount. Servers and bar team receive ten points, back servers three and a half or five, depending on whether they bus or serve or both. The hostess receives two and a half. Tonight these are sizeable amounts and will be added to everyone's biweekly paycheck.

Saturday morning, though, is different. The atmosphere lacks the animated efficiency of a busy service. Brunch has not caught on. On this late-summer morning there are four tables (amounting to all of ten people) reserved. Lien is running as lean a shift as she can. Lena, a server, places cutlery on the tables. Hayden, a culinary student in a French bulldog T-shirt, works as back server and fills pitchers with iced water. Jorge, who also works at a newly launched downtown restaurant, will be mixing drinks. Jonathan is taking the morning off, and James, an old friend from the Animal days, will jump onto the line to assist the two cooks if it gets busy. It probably won't. Jonathan and Lien have thought about why. Koreatown and HLAY are perceived as nighttime destinations. Though just so no one can say you can only get coconut waffles with koji whipped cream here, Jonathan had adapted the menu to offer sunny-side up or scrambled eggs, toasts, and date-sugar-crusted grapefruit brûlée—dishes that honor the comforts of brunch but allow the restaurant's culinary identity to shine through. It's tough-going. "I've reached out to journalists about brunch," Lien says, "and no one has gotten back to me."

Still, the time is hardly being wasted. Jorge has an affable nature and a sharp, decisive turn of a shaker that speaks of experience. He's excited to have picked up one more dinner shift at HLAY and doesn't mind having to drop one at the other restaurant where he works. Hayden is gaining dining room experience, a valuable addition to her résumé if she becomes a chef. Kelly is training to be the supervisor for the shift. She is wearing a wide-sleeved shirt and high-waisted salvage denim jeans that lend her movements a certain swagger, though she joins the group gathered at the corner of the bar for preshift discreetly, as one of the team. After going over a few drinks specials, Lien ends the gathering with a reminder of what will happen next. "It can be awkward when a crew member gets promoted because they are now asking you to do things," she says. "The most helpful thing you can do for Kelly right now is just do anything she asks." Kelly looks a little bashful; Lena gives a few excited claps.

Kelly's promotion means a few responsibilities are taken off Lien. Each shift has certain tasks such as detailing dishes that were taken off a check—comped—and briefly explaining why it was done. Kelly has never had that kind of responsibility before, and back at the hostess stand she considers the moment. "It's going to be interesting to understand what everybody else is doing. It's good to see it from Lien's point of view." A few minutes later two young parents with a small child enter. They're walk-ins, or the high chair they request would already have been placed at the table. "Just let me get your table ready," Kelly says as she quickly goes for the high chair. Within a minute, she leads them to the table by the window as she asks them how their day is going. Things are looking up. The guest count has already increased.

You CAN HIRE PEOPLE and let them fail, or you can set them up for success—both theirs and yours. Which is why successful restaurateurs are also educators. Training takes many forms, but whether it's organizing kitchen seminars, role-playing customer interactions, or arranging vendor workshops, allowing your employees to learn and grow is a wise investment that pays dividends in terms of a better workplace environment, better consumer experience, and less staff turnover. Experienced operators let their commitment to excellence trickle down from the top.

There are two important parts to this kind of enlightened training. One is operational; the second is cultural. In the restaurant industry you learn by doing. There are schools, of course, teaching various elements of hospitality, in addition to contributing a little confidence, and these often provide the entry point to the business. But the real learning happens at the stove under pressure or tableside with a guest. Donato Poto, the co-owner of Providence, recalls his strict, old-fashioned method of Italian training in the 1970s. That meant that as a teenage student at the hospitality school in Paestum he was judged on how firmly the foam cap remained on a tray of cappuccinos as he raced across a long hallway. Later, as a dining commis, or junior assistant, in a Central London hotel, he had his eyes blindfolded while being taught to artfully carve ducks tableside. "It's dark in the dining room," he says. "Your knife has to *feel* the bones." Later, the café au lait–colored dinner jacket he wore at the Villa d'Este on Lake Como marked him as a captain but did not give him the permission to initiate a conversation at table. That kind of solemnity might seem dated today, but it was still a "value" being passed down.

At HLAY, new dining room employees undertake a series of training shifts (called *"stage,"* a word borrowed from French). Lien and Jonathan always begin with this operational part of training. The new employee trails someone in their position for several shifts. This is followed by a reverse trail, in which the new employee takes the lead while being observed by the crew member, who then reports to Lien. Then comes an extensive written test of the menu. The crew member comes in, sits at a table in the empty dining room, and describes the ingredients of every dish, down to the three chiles that go into the salsa negra draping the deep-fried, lime-splashed frog legs. "You don't go onto the floor until you've passed it," Lien says. A recent hostess candidate answered her test so well, it is taped to the office door. If all works out, the new employee can look forward to seeing their name on the schedule Lien sends out to the crew members as a jpeg every two weeks.

Teaching culture? That's a little harder to quantify. New challenges come up daily. For now, Lien's close enough to day-to-day operations that she hopes to train by example, as she does with teaching operations, rather than a manual. When a unique situation presents itself, she takes lead. Employees know how to handle a situation by watching how she does it; they'll learn values by seeing how she acts. That kind of allegiance is hard to disregard. "She's worked a shift for me," Drew says. But it is also a level of involvement that can be draining. "There are days I don't want to inspire. I don't want to always give interesting advice for you to go home and ponder," she said to no one in particular on one occasion. "I want to be given interesting advice for me to go home and ponder." Even if she could keep her energy up, demonstrating how every situation should be handled becomes impossible once a restaurateur is responsible for more than one dining room.

It took Danny Meyer a full ten years to find this out. By then he was running not just Union Square Café but also Gramercy Tavern, the restaurant he opened with Tom Colicchio in 1994. A guest had complained about an order of salmon. Since the fish was fine and she'd eaten half of it, the manager had decided not to take it off the check, but receiving what she'd left in a to-go container had struck the guest as a passive-aggressive move. She'd written to complain. "Until then, hospitality had been no more than a personal instinct," Meyer recalls thinking. "I hadn't articulated to myself what hospitality meant—or, for that matter, what the absence of hospitality meant. How could I possibly have been explicit about it to anyone else? These were the initial days of my becoming a two-restaurant restaurateur, and for the first nine years of Union Square Café's existence, I had always been on hand to see and fix things as they were happening—demonstrating what to do rather than teaching others how or why to do it. I had never had to codify how particular mistakes or crises should be addressed."

In a restaurant, there are always crises. There are equipment malfunctions that the customers shouldn't know about, air-conditioning problems invariably during heat spells. There are spilled trays, forgotten reservations, allergic reactions. Spend enough time in restaurants and you see things you never thought you would. A guest who charges into a kitchen to discuss the finer differentiations between medium rare and medium directly with the chef. A doggie bag set on fire by the tabletop candle burning unnoticed in a full dining room. Teaching culture helps employees solve crises because they will problem-solve with the values of an establishment in mind.

A crisis can even serve to motivate. Such was the case at Rossoblu, a big open restaurant located in the crowded streets of the Los Angeles fashion district. Two brief months after opening their homage to Bologna, chef Steve Samson and his wife, Dina, realized they had to make a change—and fast. "We were hiring people and it wasn't working out," Dina says, sitting at a table on the restaurant's terrace. It's the day after a busy Mother's Day. "We started to realize that some people weren't fitting in, but how can you explain that to them, that they're not going to fit, unless A, you have your core values up front; B, screen for those core values; C, reward on those core values; D, get rid of people on those core values, making changes to your team. We were going so fast, we were bringing team members in without screening them as well as we should have. And then all of a sudden we said, OK, stop, let's put the brakes on. Let's talk about it and really be conscious about who we really want to be, and who we really want to be here with us."

Despite the high stakes, the process of articulating their message was relatively simple. The Samsons, their business partner and director of hospitality Hans Luttmann, and their general partner Kevin Napoli spent several days huddled in front of a whiteboard writing down values. "Hans was reading this book called *Traction*, and basically we all stood in a room and said, 'Let's describe our core values,'" Dina recalls. "We started with Steve—creativity, inspiring, all these touchy-feely things. Then we did Hans. We were going to take the top four or five and see which ones were the same."

Luttmann, a one-time writer and actor who moved to full-time restaurant management a decade ago and has worked in several high-end restaurants in Los Angeles and New York, knew the pitfalls of writing down values. He'd experienced ostensible "cultures," restaurants so revolved around an individual that they became what he terms "hero worship." "This whole process," he recalls jokingly, "is born from pain." Still, that experience was valuable in leading them to terms that resonated. "There were thirty words up on the board, and we started to combine them. Is it empathy, or is it compassion? Does 'work ethic' mean the same thing as 'curiosity'? We wanted to get it down to four to six, and we ended up getting it down to four terms, which are 'work ethic,' 'a commitment to excellence,' 'integrity,' 'compassion.'"

"Compassion" isn't a word you often hear in the restaurant industry, which is, after all, a business where you divide labor by revenue to know where you stand. But it should be. It acknowledges the grind of service. And the fact that the human capital is as important as the financial capital required to run a restaurant. Surrounded by three-ring binders and clipboards, a manager in a back office says good night to his kids, two little figures in pajamas squirming on the screen of the phone propped on his desk. A dishwasher who's overcome the nightly wave of incoming plates cracks the back door open to feel the breeze in an alley. A waitress who one moment is crouched over with back spasms straightens up slowly, pats the order pad in her apron pocket, checks her lipstick on the chrome side of the espresso machine, and a moment later is greeting guests with a cheerful "How are you doing, folks?" What's an experience to the guest is a job to the restaurant worker. One they might prepare for with a protein shake, steel themselves for with a new set of insoles, and recover from on their days off.

"We have mantras," Luttmann says. "One of them is 'We get to take care of the restaurant, we get to take care of one another, and we get to take care of the guest.' Another mantra is 'Our food knowledge is fierce, our wine knowledge is sharp, and our capacity for love is outstanding.' And it's that third one that usually wakes the staff up. They know they have to have food knowledge and wine knowledge, but before they might say, 'I didn't know it was my job that my capacity to love had to be outstanding.' But now they know that and they embrace that." The challenge for Luttmann and the Samsons, in fact, has not been the articulation of values but the consistent integration of those values into daily operations. "It requires the discipline and focus of consistent messaging," he says. "The benefits of having these values are constant inspiration for leadership, consistency for staff, and clarity for everyone." And by "everyone" he means everyone. "I'll have servers who'll see me in a moment of consternation and then they'll say, 'How's your capacity for love right now?' And I'll say, 'Outstanding.' And I get wakened.

And that's part of taking care of one another. They take care of us more than we take care of them, to be honest."

There's something ironic in the fact that after all the vision, the money-raising, the detail, and the articulation of culture, the implementation is up to people who might be totally committed to the restaurant or might well be thinking of it as just a gig. It makes the focus on training a crucial step. Jerry Garbus, the director of operations and wine director of chef David LeFevre's Manhattan Beach restaurants, puts it clearly: "You have to build the training," he says. "It has to be there for the crew. These are the people that are going to be in front of your tables, serving your guests, and there's no substitute for that. Unless an owner is prepared to greet, seat, serve, cook, carry the food, continue to maintain the table, run the check, and usher out every single guest that walks through the door, you'd better sure as hell have great people."

Both LeFevre and Garbus learned the importance of team performance early on—LeFevre as a member of Wisconsin youth orchestras and collegiate soccer player, Garbus as a Cub Scout in a San Fernando Valley troop, and later serving as an army cavalry scout for several years before he entered the restaurant business. Garbus's first job was as a busboy at P.F. Chang's; eight years later he was GM of the Water Grill, a destination seafood restaurant in downtown LA, where he began working with LeFevre. When they set out to open M.B. Post, named because the site was originally a post office, they put the same care into the human capital end of the venture as they were putting into any of the other pressing needs. Working in a cramped office above the former barbecue joint that they were transforming into an open, high-ceilinged venue—they called it a "social house"—the two men set about the hard work of articulating their future restaurant's culture. "We sat at this table that was too big for any other use. We'd be playing tunes that maybe would go on the playlist, Jerry would play one and we'd discuss, then I'd play one," LeFevre recalls. At the same time some principles they believed in started being scratched out on legal pads and clarified on laptops—a commitment to the guest, to ingredients, to the community, and to the crew.

The collection of principles they came up with is lean enough that it can be memorized, broad enough that it encompasses all the possible circumstances that can happen in a restaurant. Under six categories—Guest, Service, Product, Atmosphere, Community, and Team—the list represents what LeFevre and Garbus call the "moral compass" that serves to guide the business of the everyday. At Fishing with Dynamite, the Nantucket-style clam shack, the cook working the oyster bar can hold forth about the difference between

East and West Coast oysters—"The *virginicas* are flatter than the *gigas*," he says using the scientific classifications—while shucking an assortment for an iced platter. That's the result of training about product. On those mornings when a team of volunteers from the restaurants (LeFevre and Garbus among them) descends on a beach to clean it up, that's the result of a commitment to the community.

Not that things stay in the higher reaches of culture. Running throughout the training material is the real nuts-and-bolts stuff of daily operations. Garbus leads all new service employees through a demanding, eight-hour-per-day, six-day training session that in addition to service standards and the entire wine and cocktail list gets into the nitty-gritty of things. What's the correct way to inform a guest their credit card has been declined? The steps a barkeep should follow before cutting someone off (as well as the disciplinary ones a team member should expect if they are habitually late)? And what exactly should you do when the guest doesn't like the $800 bottle of 1964 Barolo they requested from the reserve list? At the three restaurants they operate today, functional and cultural training aspects are so interwoven that they often occur side by side. In the big, airy dining room of M.B. Post, a beverage vendor's brand ambassador holds a tasting of prime Japanese single malts for the bar team, while upstairs, in a paper-goods storage room, a manager and a newly hired sous-chef undergoing training role-play a scene with an imaginary guest who feels rushed because instead of the dessert menu he received the check. "Acknowledge, acknowledge," says chef Ray Hayashi, who is acting as the senior manager observing the interaction and giving feedback. "Don't go straight into save mode. The guy is pissed."

To spend some time with restaurateurs is to appreciate the focus they place on thorough training. During mock service training at Providence in Hollywood, Donato often finds himself overseeing the kind of exchange between a server and teammate, in the role of a customer, that he was never allowed. His goal is to set a tone of friendliness that stops short of cutting into the time the guests have together. Meanwhile in Pasadena, at the fourth location of his Mercado restaurants, Jesse Gomez is breaking down the aguas frescas for his newly hired crew. Jesse grew up in El Arco Iris, the modest neighborhood Mexican restaurant his family ran for over fifty years in the Highland Park neighborhood. His SAT scores (and the three-pointer he developed at South Pasadena High) got him into Princeton. On his phone he can quickly access complex leases with common-area maintenance fees he negotiates with mall operators, he can also look at estimates for construction and kitchen design proposals, but today he is intent on bridging a language divide. Standing before the crew who in a few days will go live, he breaks down trickier words—spending plenty of time on "*mole Oaxaqueño*"—for English speakers who may not have worked in a Mexican restaurant before. "If someone asks for *piña*, that's pineapple," he says as the group takes notes.

Like Jesse, Lien often focuses training on product knowledge, which provides insights for the servers to tap into when standing tableside. Knowing details leads to confidence and to increased sales. The staff all clock in for every hour-and-a-half training session, significantly increasing the labor cost for the day—a sign of Lien's commitment. Still, there they are sitting around several dining room tables that have been arranged into a single long one, discussing a little-known Italian varietal or how well the rounded acidity of riesling goes with Jonathan's spicy yet creamy and lush food. On another occasion they take up the bar stools as two of the barmen mix all the new cocktails—a gorgeous collection of hues, glassware, and types of ice—and pass them along with recyclable straws for each crew member to taste. "Mmm," Drew moans as he sips one called Arturo's Case, a colorful, just-shaken tumbler of Oaxacan espadin mezcal tickled with lime juice and hibiscus-pineapple syrup. "I'd give my number to that drink!"

5

ENTREPRENEUR

Of all the types of dining establishments out there, the coffee shop is the one where Lien might feel most at ease. It doesn't mean she won't do the full tasting menu with wine pairings somewhere or that she won't hunt down a place where the fermentation jars sit on the shelves. And for a great burger she will travel far. But maybe it's memories of all those post-football-game gatherings at TGI Fridays and Chili's as an Atlanta teen that make her comfortable and knowledgeable about come-as-you-are popular spots. She'll do the combo at Denny's near HLAY. The tofu scramble gets picked at the Brite Spot diner in Echo Park. At House of Pies in Los Feliz, she orders the corned beef hash with two eggs, pancakes, and, why not, a side of bacon.

This morning she has come to Destroyer, a newish venture that serves as something of a commissary for a cluster of creative businesses that have settled amid industrial warehouses in Culver City on LA's Westside. Executives taking meetings here wear sneakers, and the menu—projected on a wall rather than printed on paper—reflects a Nordic sensibility, with heritage grains and cultured-milk products assembled in hand-thrown bowls. Lien is at an outside table, a number before her. She is hungry enough that she's looking forward to the Icelandic rye bread with cultured butter, but she is also doing research. One thing she is looking at is counter service. The economics make sense because you go without servers and only require people to run food to the tables, like the one she is sitting at. But she also wonders if counter service limits sales because a good server can encourage guests to explore a menu. From her table on the crowded terrace, she looks at people shuffling toward the counter to place their order. "At the iPad it's a very short time to create that sparkle."

When asked, though, if the tip amounts suggested by the payment screen seem high for a counter-service eatery (they are 18, 20, and 25 percent), she explains it from the operator's point of view. And she certainly doesn't object. Looking around, she says, "A normal person who's not in the business won't know, but that tip went to that guy, that girl, the iPad person, and the coffee maker, and maybe even the kitchen depending on their models."

The food world is often a prism for large social issues. The sit-ins that occurred at the Woolworth lunch counter in Greensboro, North Carolina, in 1960 were an important moment in advancing the cause and perception of racial integration. Today's conversations are about sexual harassment, gentrification, cultural appropriation, and identity. In an age of homelessness, it falls to restaurants—often fast-food restaurants—to provide bathrooms to an unhoused and undervalued population. At a time of heightened environmental awareness, operational materials such as Styrofoam containers and straws become important parts of broader campaigns. If it's being talked about on the street, it's being acted on in restaurants. When Lien makes even a glancing remark about tips, it's because for her it is real and her version of a restaurant has some kind of parity between front and back of house. Historically, front-of-the-house staff earns more because of the tipping system. The back of the house, the cooks in particular, can sometimes overlook this, understanding they are working toward a career as they advance their skills. But increases in the minimum wage mean structural systems have to be rethought. In Lien's mind it is a necessity. "If you want people to be there helping you during your meal," she says, "it has to be."

With that in mind she and Jonathan are exploring having

a flat service charge at the new restaurant. Representing a higher percentage of the check than the 3 percent "kitchen love" an operator might suggest to supplement the salary of kitchen workers, this larger amount would be distributed to both front and back of the house instead of tips. The method would, for example, augment the salary of a worthy line cook whose hourly rate couldn't reasonably be increased above $15 an hour. Her goal for all her future workers is for them to have real financial stability that allows them to live and raise families in the neighborhood they work in. Because she's a restaurateur, figuring out how to make it happen is on her list of things to do.

In many ways Lien and Jonathan have reached a juncture that all successful restaurateurs come to. You've mastered what it takes to open and operate one restaurant. You got that great review, made the list, and business is growing. How about another? The opportunities certainly abound. But how do you keep the challenges and your own doubts in perspective and instead use your hard-won knowledge to increase the chances of capturing lightning in a bottle twice?

At this moment, a successful second launch seems like something far in the future. What Lien has right now, sitting amid the creative types in this Culver City spot, is a playful, swaggy name for the new business: All Day Baby. She also has the location on Sunset Boulevard in Silver Lake and the concept, a loose riff on a drop-in-anytime diner. What she doesn't have is two-thirds of the $1.25 million she's thinking it will take to get the place going. And if that wasn't bad enough, she's now being watched. In 2016, she and Jonathan opened HLAY in stealth mode, and took the time they needed to sharpen the cooking, tighten procedures, get their footing, and find their clientele. But Eater, a popular food website, has already mentioned All Day Baby in a post, and that gets people, random people she meets at parties, wanting to talk about it. "I met people the other day," she says, eyeing the last bite of Icelandic rye bread, "and they wanted to talk all high concept and, what's the word, *lofty*." She takes a bite. "Really?"

For someone who is determinedly cheery, the change of tone, even if momentary, is noticeable. Lien will laugh about her usual disposition, saying, "I can only work with happy people or they'll find me insufferable." Her taste for diners and spicy hot wings, her pealing laugh, her memory of people's names and residual Southern charm that conjures up the term "visiting" are all part of her positive energy. It's an enthusiasm that makes her crew respect her, which makes customers value the moments she spends with them, and which, as her profile grows, puts demands on her time. At a program on women in the food industry held at the Skirball Cultural Center she was in full swing: She brought a salad with hamachi, puffed wild rice, and fried almonds for the crowd to nibble, as well as chilled bottles of *pét-nat* for them to sip. She captivated the large audience as she recalled the four meals the late legendary critic Jonathan Gold had at the restaurant before he wrote his review. "On the fourth visit I knew he was going to order the rib eye," she says. "He had to."

Momentary though it may be, this recent shift in attitude is due to a series of difficult moments occurring within weeks of each other. The first was a customer pushing a hostess when Lien wasn't there. The carefully scheduled reservation times had been thrown off when the hostess squeezed in a party of six, and failed to tell this party of the exact time of the next reservation. The margin for error disappeared when some of the first party unknowingly trailed in late. And the crisis erupted two hours later. Ordinarily Lien has techniques for getting a table back. One is to keep offering to refill water glasses; there's something about such focus on the table that makes folks realize there are people waiting. As a last resort she will apologetically ask for the table—offering a drink at the bar if there's any room. Getting a table back from a lingering party is one of the most awkward moments in the business.

That night, Lien, taking a rare night off, had left before the trouble began. She only got to read about it in the closing-shift notes at one in the morning when she returned home. The push that had perhaps or perhaps not been intentional came as the first party departed. The manager on duty had felt powerless. The hostess had cried in the office. Lien spent a sleepless night wondering whether to call and confront the party to defend her staff but remained unsure if the push was intentional. "This table 41 could haunt me forever if I don't attend to it," she'd said. "At the end of the day am I going to reach out to the guest and remind them of it? I'm not sure." She'd paused. Her own well-being was part of the equation also. "But I have to let it go. Chef tells me all the time I have to let shit go." After talking it over with the crew, she had decided not to call. Days later it was still hard to shake this one off.

Less raw, though no less challenging, is the drawn-out planning process for All Day Baby. Lien must go through a community-review process before being granted certain important permits. A few weeks earlier she, together with Eddie Navarrette, the All Day Baby representative, appeared at the monthly meeting of the Silver Lake Neighborhood

Council's Urban Design and Preservation Advisory Committee. The group's recommendations affect subsequent decisions made by the LA Department of City Planning, and this is an early and important step in the permit process. Meetings are held inside a recreation center whose outside basketball court is a favorite neighborhood spot for pickup games. Inside there's a court, too, and for this meeting folding metal chairs for the public and long folding-leg tables for the committee members were set up on the hardwood, the layout suggesting, if not adversity, at least two different teams.

The tone was set early with a developer's request to fit ten modernist town houses into a weirdly angled lot. The incline of the driveway, the manicuring of the street front, and the apparent dullness of the design were all discussed before the project was sent back for revisions. A restaurateur with a popular beer bar who wanted to extend the hours he could serve alcohol was up next. His project manager projected a Google Earth image of the surrounding streets on a roll-down screen and highlighted every house and business on the street that had approved the hours. He'd gone door-to-door and secured their signatures. He introduced a transgender woman who vouched for the owner and said how the diverse community benefited from fund-raisers held at the venue. The conversation barely touched on either of these endorsements, quickly homing in on how noise travels up canyons. There are lots of canyons in that part of Silver Lake. He was told to return with revised hours.

Then it was Lien's turn to stand before the panel. She wore a lavender windbreaker with a barking Doberman on the back. Perhaps it was how its oversized design draped her, but she seemed small, the spark she could bring to a dining room muted by the dampness of the gym. The discussion for the new restaurant soon turned to noise. All Day Baby is not a business that masks its intentions, and several committee members pointed to it as a problem. "It's in your name!" one of them said. A fit professorial couple in black and gray who lived directly behind the project wanted to know about the patio. None of the restaurants that had occupied the corner spot before had served food there. Navarrette explained that the final designs weren't yet in place. The conversation turned to cars. The location had three staff parking spaces behind the building and one curbside space they'd probably be reserving for pickup orders. "This plan is absurd," said one committee member. "You need parking." Lien replied they were working out details with a valet parking company. There was some grumbling that this was all vague, though something of a reply to that point came up when a man spoke from the back with the pointed tone of a gadfly. "You guys are showing how out of touch you are with all this talk of parking," he said to the committee. "People take Uber."

Throughout it all Lien maintained the look she might if a customer had called her over to say a dish was too salty. Concerned, not code blue. Perhaps it was knowing that discussing parking alternatives in a restaurant that didn't have funding, a staff, or a menu and hadn't in fact even broken ground seemed premature. Still, this was a procedural step and a necessary one and, indeed, part of the ever-changing definition of being a restaurateur. Back in those distant midcentury *Mad Men* days, RA's Joe Baum might have foretold the future when he grasped that a restaurateur didn't risk anonymity (his profile in the *New Yorker* appeared in 1964) by refusing to play the host. With her growing confidence, Lien understood that in addition to parrying objections, scheduling meetings, and establishing next steps, she was also the chief attraction. It wasn't all that surprising after the meeting broke up, as she, Navarrette, and the couple concerned with noise were talking in the glow of the outside basketball court, when one of the committee members came up to her. "I've heard all about Here's Looking at You," he said. "I can't wait to go."

———

THE GADFLY (IF THAT was his role) was onto something when he mentioned the constantly shifting ways of public behavior. Restaurateurs are, after all, in the service industry, and they must constantly modify their offerings to suit changing demands. Entire modes of thinking can suddenly disappear—think of how dining rooms transformed from tablecloths and glasses with stems to live-edged communal tables and tumblers. Restaurateurs are constantly finding ways to modify the experience, especially now with respect to technology.

A restaurateur might be alternating between established and innovative methods. Josiah Citrin, a native Angeleno, has separate approaches at his two West LA restaurants. At Michelin-starred Mélisse in Santa Monica, the waitstaff use cordless irons to steam the creases out of heavy cotton tablecloths, the champagne cart is stocked with the finest blanc de blancs, and servers deliver the plates in unison like the chorus in a ballet. Nearby, on the ground floor of a short-term rental apartment building in Venice, Citrin operates the far more relaxed Charcoal, a steak house designed around the backyard art of grilling. Here, the waitstaff place orders tableside, thumbs and fingers moving quickly as they enter dishes, drinks, and modifications into handheld devices. Orders fly out from a giant Big Green Egg grill and land on bare wood tables. Moving between the two restaurants in a single evening, Citrin might go from wearing his white chef's jacket on a goodwill tour of the dining room to being the guy in a T-shirt clearing the Bird scooters cluttering his doorway.

"Charcoal runs really smooth," he says at his Venice bungalow home on a day off. "It was set up to run smooth. I tried to think it out and it worked. I tried to make a concept that was going to work. A concept that wasn't too progressive or too fancy. It's not too hard to reproduce and keep doing. The line being five people, I really thought about it in a financial way also. I just happened to get lucky. It worked pretty much as I thought it was going to."

That ability to conceive and execute a concept is different from when he first opened Mélisse in 1999. He'd prepared for the starring chef-owner role in a multitude of restaurants. And he still remembers them in characteristic chef fashion by the dishes each kitchen put out. Wolfgang Puck's Chinois on Main in the mid '80s? "That was the duck fried rice." Joachim Splichal's Patina on Melrose Avenue in 1992? "That was the scallop rolls hot out of the pan with brown-butter balsamic, that Santa Barbara shrimp with the mashed potatoes and truffle chips, the lamb gratin."

From the start, Mélisse was wildly ambitious. Josiah spent $100,000 on a brand-new Garland center-suite stove. Whatever he had left went toward laying down cases of great burgundy. In the dining room there was tableside veal chop, Dover sole with a tumble of herb-flecked chanterelles, and a rolling cheese cart—but still, he was at the mercy of other forces, too. With a laugh, the fifty-one-year-old, who still moves with the nimbleness of a lifelong surfer, remembers early coverage. "The *LA Times* praised our rotisserie chicken, and suddenly I had to go out and buy a whole bunch of rotisseries because that was *our* dish."

Those were days when newspaper food sections ruled, when an early-model sous vide device and an answering machine represented technology. These days technology suffuses the restaurant business, both in the kitchen and the dining room. Reservations systems like OpenTable and Resy can keep track of when you last dined and when—pang of conscience—you last no-showed. Managers can check these reservations on their phones, and then decide how much staff they need for the evening. In a world of scarce line cooks, a chef's Instagram feed is a recruiting tool: "This is how we throw down here!" Charcoal, in particular, has been adept at using these shifting methods. In fact, for a while Citrin and his chef de cuisine, Joseph Johnson, appeared on billboards for the food-delivery app Grubhub. It made for a good picture: Citrin, the weathered surfer whose mom was a caterer, and Johnson, an African-American chef whose mom worked the front desk of the Virginia hotel where he got his start. Both looked straight at the camera with a look that communicated you'd be missing out if you didn't have them deliver something grilled over coals to your home.

Even given the efficiency of online reservation systems, these food-delivery apps may be the most significant technological tool to enter the restaurant equation. They have the ability to help restaurateurs increase revenue and thus lower labor cost. It's why the ping that announces an incoming order is heard in ever more kitchens. "We try to package it in a way that they can't mess it up. Just the way we stack it in the bags, so it's all secure inside," Josiah says of the danger of the food not arriving in a way that's representative of the restaurant. It's crucial that the food is up to customers' expectations. It's a risk for every restaurateur—not every driver arrives with the thermal bag they're supposed to; others pause to try and sneak a beer at the bar. Josiah is wary enough that he asks friends to place orders and report on how they arrive. Still, despite the commission (usually between 20 and 30 percent), the benefits are overwhelming: additional sales that don't require additional staff. "I'm get-

ting business that I can't fit in the restaurant at that time,"
Josiah says as he turns to his phone screen to share some figures. "So I do $3,000 in a week, they take $800, then I have
$2,200 and it cost me 30 percent, 35 with all the packaging
and all that, so I have profit there. Found money, money
that doesn't exist somewhere else." The figures appear
quickly and he reels them off. "For the last week Uber Eats
was $750, Grubhub $950, Postmates was $1,200, Caviar was
$450. When it gets too busy, we turn it off. When it gets to
be eight o'clock and the tickets are pouring in, I need to take
care of the customers in the restaurant. That's what's great,
you can turn it off and on. I never thought I'd be doing anything like this."

Lien and Jonathan also aim to take full advantage of the
new sources of income food apps represent, though they'll
ease into them so as to not throw off the rhythm of the
kitchen. In fact, from the start, Lien has conceived of All
Day Baby with all the new ways people enjoy restaurants in
mind. "Takeout counter, food to grab & go, coffee pickup
window"—the twenty-four-page business proposal offers
many ways to serve food other than sitting down in a dining room. The space, in a former Indian restaurant, is located in a neighborhood that is changing—there are body
shops and seafood taco stands, but there is also a vegan shoe

store a block away. Still, Samosa House is not an institution being displaced; it's a venture that didn't make it. Lien and Jonathan heard about it from a contractor, came to see it, loved the scale, the high ceiling, the pocket-sized patio, and the corner location that let in plenty of light. Lien writes her proposals with plenty of verve, and this one is no different. She speaks passionately about the needs of the neighborhood, pulling in suppositions, acknowledging the way people eat. It's a love letter to a place that welcomes you and that plays a central place in your life. "What is this modern Silver Laker eating?" she asks. "Is he or she interested in flavor? Of course! What about flair? Imagine a cute lil' spot that feels like it has its own personality that feels good to be in? We're wondering: Does this person have to leave Silver Lake in order to go somewhere 'cool' and 'special' to celebrate a great occasion? And finally, what about flexibility? Can't there be more than just wings and mixed-green salads on Postmates?"

She continues: "We ask: Where is a grown-up Silver Laker supposed to go for a unique experience—that's not an ordeal!—on a Monday night or a Thursday morning or a lazy Sunday afternoon—to have a satisfying meal? And, yes, with adult beverages. The modern Silver Lake diner craves flavor, demands flair, and needs flexibility."

It's interesting to note the similarities and the differences between the proposals for HLAY and All Day Baby. Both are written with Lien's cheery voice; both include highly detailed financial projections. Both have pictures of a neighborhood iconic image on the cover; for All Day Baby, the image of the Wiltern theater is supplanted by an iconic neighborhood sign that reads "Sunset Junction." Immediate differences jump out: In the first proposal, Lien and Jonathan provided detailed résumés; for this project they are "the Founders of HLAY." Their record of accomplishment now speaks for itself. Instead of spending time on bios, Lien has extended her version of market analysis. Whereas for Here's Looking at You, she nodded to existing restaurants such as Roy Choi's Commissary and Gary Menes's Le Comptoir but concentrated on describing the sense of movement in Koreatown, for All Day Baby she analyzes the competition under the specific categories. Some have brunch, some have cocktails, none have it all, making All Day Baby unique.

The proposal shows Jonathan's growing versatility, too, adapting his style to blue plate specials like Saturday's brunch short rib migas with eggs, and Friday's meat loaf with mashed potatoes, green beans, and shiitake mushroom gravy. The proposed menu has hotcakes with pistachio ricotta, and the roasted cauliflower on baguette with whipped tahini and mint sounds appealing. There are eggs, of course, and pork links and *pain de mie* toast with seasonal jam that honor the diner concept. But Jonathan and Lien are wary of being too obvious about their inspiration. Jonathan puts it in his direct manner: "That place with '57 Chevy crap all over the walls. That's what I don't want." Lien is more conceptual: "I think what's worth mentioning is we're talking about the inspiration being a diner, but I actually think once we open we won't talk about it again. The inspiration behind Jonathan's crisp veal sweetbreads with pickled fennel dish is McDonald's chicken nuggets dipped in sweet-and-sour sauce, but that's not something we need to disclose to the guest. The journey for the guest, and why they call dinner an experience, is they need to find these things for themselves. So I think the same thing is when people come in to All Day Baby, their immediate reaction might be this is a diner or they are just going to see it as a place they can hit up every day if they want to, maybe every other day, or do it in different formats because they have lives and kids and they'll gladly pay for somebody to make dinner for them but it doesn't have to be an ordeal." This is how restaurateurs get good: They can see one detail from many perspectives—the chef, the servers, the guests, and so on. Seeing things from others' point of view is part of Lien's plan today.

One morning, Lien and Jonathan drive down to Sunset Beach, south of the Port of Los Angeles, to visit the Harbor House Café, a twenty-four-hour, decades-old diner Jonathan used to visit as a child. In some ways, working together has made them like a married couple. They don't quite finish each other's sentences, but they talk in shorthand and allow comfortable—and, when called for, even uncomfortable—long silences to settle between them. Also, Jonathan can't wait for Lien to catch up on her viewing of *The Crown*, the Netflix series centered around the British royal family, so they can discuss. "Do you have the clicker?" Jonathan asks before they even leave the gated parking area behind HLAY. "My clicker never works." Within minutes they are heading out of Koreatown in Jonathan's early-model Prius. The streetscape of the city, with all its tangled intersections, graffitied warehouses, and pallet yards, soon gives way to the smooth swoosh of the freeway.

This outing is also a bit of an escape, as if leaving Los Angeles allows them to forget the pressures they are under. Earlier in the week a sizeable investment group dropped out of All Day Baby. Even for Lien, who has learned to differentiate between a verbal commitment and financial one, this was a shock—and a reminder of how messy fund-raising can be. They are already paying $12,655.90 every month in rent.

The kitchen equipment—the smoker, the range, and the hood alone—will come to $200,000, and they have made a down payment. They decided to move a shear wall in the space, an action that required untangling the mess of pipes that straggle down from upstairs apartments. "We've spent $400,000 on stuff you cannot see," Jonathan says, listing expenses while driving. "The architect, the general contractor, permits, opening escrow on a liquor license. Honestly, City of LA has gotten most of our checks."

There are only a certain amount of those liquor licenses in Los Angeles at any one time, and though there is a yearly lottery for a handful, the best way to acquire one is to do it, like they have, through a broker. Even so, the price can be well over $100,000—frightening enough to many new operators that they will go instead with the far less onerous beer-and-wine license, which is only a few thousand dollars. Lien and Jonathan, however, see being able to offer cocktails as a key part of the way they operate, liquor sales helping as a draw, as an image, to create atmosphere, enhance food, and increase revenue.

It's not hard to understand why. The industry average for liquor cost hovers between 12 and 15 percent, and that's even lower if the operator has been able to establish good terms by getting in early on a new release or agreeing to use a significant amount of product in a signature cocktail. Either way, spending $14 to make $100 is the kind of handsome margin that can make a well-run bar a necessity. With its rubber mats, burnished wood counter, and brass rail, the American bar is mostly laid out in a way that any barkeep can step behind and quickly get to work. Clear spirits go on the right, so vodka and gin give way to rum, tequila, triple sec, bourbon, whiskey, and, on the far left, Scotch. The highballs, parasol-crowned mugs, and frosted martinis they produce become a key part in a restaurant's business plan.

Given a bar's ability to generate profit, it's tempting to think of it as nothing but a handsome revenue stream. But to progressive restaurateurs, liquor sales are more complex, central even to their approach. For Gomez, that Princeton grad who went back into the family business, a busy bar is a way to generate an animated atmosphere that leads to increased food sales, and even a way to come home. Without the additional income from the bar, he might not have chosen to put his grandmother's slow-simmered El Arco Iris chile verde recipe on his Pasadena menu when the restaurant opened. In a similar way, the profit from liquor sales at All Day Baby won't just contribute to the bottom line; it'll provide a buffer for Jonathan to experiment with ingredients and offset an occasional splurge. If Lien goes with the flat-service-charge idea, cocktail sales will provide higher sales and ultimately a higher amount of dollars to be distributed among the crew. The person putting extra work into prepping in the early morning will be there in part because of the chilled manhattans served at night.

Soon the freeway off-ramp has given way to a stretch of coastline where a navy yard and retirement community line opposite sides of a curving two-lane road. When Harbor House Café opened in 1939, this area of Sunset Beach was dotted with working oil wells and the small diner served chow to long-haul truck drivers. The sloped-roof structure has kept the unfussy air of those times. "I used to call this place Superman," Jonathan says as he alights from the car and points at the weathered image of the superhero that rises, propelled by his clenched fist, between the restaurant's sign and the structure's striped awning. Lien, wearing pleated dark blue slacks and bright red patent leather mules, is right behind, pausing to take a picture on her phone. They head into the darkly lit place, with its nine well-used swiveling stools and recessed booths. Jonathan goes straight to the back patio, where plastic patio furniture and Christmas lights and old movie posters combine to form a timeless atmosphere.

"I used to come after school," he says, looking at the

menu and checking off classics. "Patty melt, tuna melt, the bacon avocado omelet, the biscuits and gravy, the burritos are good here. The chili cheese burger is good," he says to Lien, "but you hate chili cheese."

"I'm thinking of the hot crab sandwich," she says.

"Where's the hot crab sandwich? I've never even seen it."

"It was called out, hard-core, on the website."

"Oh, yeah, there's the hot crabmeat sandwich. It's a melt with crab. I've never even noticed that thing there. There's the Ortega burger, it's like a Southwestern burger thing. Every diner has an Ortega burger, it's like a Tex-Mex burger."

Lien, who has a quick eye for details in restaurants, looks around, taking in the room, pleased to get an insight into Jonathan. She is here to enjoy. Within a few minutes, the server has returned to take the order.

"I'd like to try your hot crabmeat sandwich," Lien says.

"Would you like that with French fries, onion rings, or coleslaw?"

"French fries."

"For you?" she asks Jonathan.

"Can I do the bacon avocado cheese omelet, hash browns, and can I add sausage to it and can I get a side of ranchero sauce."

As soon as the server is gone, he describes the sauce he's

just ordered to Lien. "Ranchero is like a thing in diners where Latin migrant workers were working, so it's peppers, onions, chiles, and tomato, and you just cook that down." He seems happy. A plastic-covered menu filled with triple-decker sandwiches and well-executed classics has the capacity to do that. It's what's excited him about creating the dishes that will be offered at All Day Baby. "I'm not even that hungry," he says of his order, "but I'm going to crush this thing."

There has been much lip-smacking during the meal, but after the plates have been cleared and the mugs refilled, Jonathan and Lien start talking business. "I think it's really hard to achieve 100 percent success by doing classics," Lien says. "Because you do go to a lot of places, a diner customer is going to be even more critical of something that they've had a perfect version of somewhere in their past."

"Yes," Jonathan agrees. "We'll always have avocado toast, a large selection of salads and dips and things like that. I think that will gravitate to a lot of our grab-and-go stuff. In the dining room I want it to be side-by-side tables where people can order these giant plates of food." He pauses to consider the restaurant in a more general way. "It's harder, this one. I'm restraining myself. It has to stay true to the original. I've got to make a patty melt without going crazy."

"I have a question about salads to go," Lien says. "Are

you going to put the dressing on the side, or are you going to dress it?"

"No, on the side, of course. Tightly packed, though. It might be in the back of some dude's car going forty-five around the curves of Silver Lake."

They share a laugh. Important as they are, the details are a way of not talking about harder subjects to address. The money that's not in the bank, for one. And more abstract questions, too: Can they capture whatever it was they captured at Here's Looking at You again—mood, mission, the excitement a new mix of flavors might create, all the imponderables that restaurateurs launch themselves toward with every project? More formidable than any of them is: Can they capture the moment? In Los Angeles that means compressing the miles of freeway, boulevard, and street into one location whose windows frame the city and our times in a new way. These epoch-defining eateries happen in LA with an unexpected rapidity. When it opened in 1982 on the Sunset Strip, Spago was a place with a haute cuisine–trained Austrian chef who was switching to wood-fired pizzas to have a little fun. Before it became a huge success, Sqirl, the place that redefined coffee-culture cuisine nationally, was where you might head for a pour-over and a jar of Jessica Koslow's dry-farmed apricot jam. Chef Ria Dolly Barbosa, one of the city's most promising talents, was the opening chef there. She found the job through a Craigslist ad a week before it opened. Space was so tight, they kept the Vitamix blender for the sorrel pesto that brightened the signature rice bowl in a snug indoor closet carved out beneath the weirdly slanted ceiling. A dozen or so customers would wander in for the toast and jam, choose a bowl, and extend their stay with a coffee. "It was like, oh, yay, we made $400 today," Barbosa recently recalled. "And it's just so funny to look back and think how exciting that moment was. It's like, oh, my God, people are actually coming, this could be something." She's talking, of course, of when the hodgepodge of thoughts and notions behind a restaurant connect in a popular way. It's so hard to create that energy Jonathan and Lien want for All Day Baby. That might be why they are just happy to eat and not talk.

From this distance, All Day Baby takes on a defining solidity; to be the center of a neighborhood, to be a place you need and want, these are worthy goals. The proposal is at its most transparent when it takes aim at those heights. "We want to offer convenience & flexibility without sacrificing taste, standards, values nor simple exhilaration," Lien writes. "This fun little restaurant will have one simple intention. To bring you joy." In this way, Lien is certainly the visionary. But without the financing secured, it is all risk. Real risk. Scary risk. "We can't fail," she says, "and it's very easy to fail as a restaurant." She is not just a visionary; she is a facilitator, too. She's a restaurateur.

As if prompted by the cheerful groups who've entered the Harbor House, Lien smiles as she looks around. It's been good to see this place, a touchstone for Jonathan, something they can take inspiration from and use to define their next project. Lien will have to think about each aspect required to launch it—the financial capital and the human capital, too—all the while making sure HLAY keeps running the way it should, without her daily oversight.

Lien and Jonathan get back in the car, and they have soon left the coastal quiet behind. They are quiet, too, as the car climbs an overpass on the Harbor Freeway, revealing LA, with the towers of downtown and the mountains behind them. It's two o'clock when they pull back into the parking lot behind Here's Looking at You. A potential investor for All Day Baby is coming in to dinner at six. As always in the restaurant business, there's so much work to be done.

CODA: VISIONARY, REDUX

All Day Baby is vacant, unoccupied, the vestiges of the restaurant it has been no more than discolored sections of wall that mark the spots that pieces of equipment used to occupy. Newly installed pipes rise a few feet from the ground and are capped. The waist-high placement indicates they are for new sinks. But is that area where the bar, the kitchen, or a bathroom will go? A large workman's toolbox sits on what is more trench than floor. To view a restaurant at such a basic state is to see it before it can go anywhere near the realm of meaning; it is held back because it hasn't reached function yet. A construction permit affixed to the inside of the door might as well be a lottery ticket. But the bones are there. Lien sees them. Even with the insulation drooping between exposed beams, the high ceiling has an airy quality that will serve to frame a dramatic room. The scale of those windows, for now hidden behind dying plants that catch every breath of hot traffic air on Sunset

Boulevard, will one day soon allow in gorgeous slanted shafts of light. Empty now, the dining room will be filled with people, laptops, and croissants in the morning, Jonathan's blue plate special—yes, that meatloaf with mashed potatoes and shiitake mushroom gravy—on Friday nights. Staff will get to know names. Guests will get to know staff. The barkeep will remember how someone likes his or her martini, perhaps the glass just rinsed with vermouth. And a server, closing out a check, will hum some well-known song when it shuffles up on the playlist. Amy Winehouse, Prince, the Strokes, they, too, will become part of the place.

By advancing and excelling, Lien has created a business but also found a path. At times she would even say a home. Lien loves how the community that develops among a restaurant team overflows and includes the guests. Becoming a place people want to head to can at times be a daily battle, but it is also a responsibility. For a moment guests are connecting, and she has played a role in that as a restaurateur. It is a unique job, one that requires having a sense of what the market wants and the tenacity to endure a long process. But before it all, a restaurateur needs the vision that can conceive of something that doesn't exist yet. This curb in front of All Day Baby, for example, that has a nice rounded width like a riverbank will one day be a great pull-in spot for the coffee pickup or the food-app driver. Rising, the pavement narrows into hills thick with Silver Lake flora, the cypresses and the towering cactuses reaching upwards amid the splash of lavender and bougainvillea. A hot wind blows up there, the kind of raw desert wind that will sometimes crack across the city. If you were to head back down these curves in six months, the first place you'd reach would be All Day Baby. It will be a good place to go. A smiling Lien will probably be welcoming guests at the door.

APPENDIX

The best way to understand how a restaurant works is to take a seat in one. Everything might not be in plain sight, but a lot of it is. You glimpse the drinks ticket being stabbed, pick up on the interactions between regulars and staff, notice when the flowers could be refreshed. When food, wine, and atmosphere work in harmony, a moment of memorable pleasure has been created. When a tray of glasses is dropped in the dining room, everyone hears it. For the person considering a career as a restaurateur, just dining out is an opportunity to explore the industry without committing to a career path.

Next, a job or even an internship or *stage* is a good first step. Maybe even a necessary one. A restaurateur needs to understand each position in a restaurant, from A to Z. There are a lot of repetitive actions in kitchens and dining rooms, and plenty of ways that things can go wrong . . . so practice makes perfect. Restaurants are a business without second takes, and guests draw conclusions very quickly. But a genuine apology can save a situation, and there's often another table waiting, with another chance to get things right. On the plus side, those who work in the trenches of hospitality are providing basic comforts in a wide variety of atmospheres, from quietly elegant to raucous fun. For many, the satisfaction of working in a lively environment and walking out with a little money in their pocket is enough motivation to stay in the industry and keep improving at their specialized tasks.

For those wishing to enter the restaurant world armed with a diploma, a wide variety of community colleges, culinary institutes, and universities have comprehensive full-time and part-time programs. Specialized schools such as the Cornell School of Hotel Administration, the Collins College of Hospitality Management at Cal Poly Pomona, and the William F. Harrah College of Hospitality at the University of Nevada, Las Vegas, as well as many others, offer both undergraduate and graduate degrees. Boston University's School of Hospitality Administration recently launched an innovative one-year Master of Management in Hospitality course designed for recent college graduates and people switching careers. The following link is a useful tool to start exploring further educational possibilities:

https://www.accreditedschoolsonline.org/culinary-schools
/restaurant-management.

Of course, there's a difference between taking a course and running a restaurant. And, while having a working knowledge of fundamental practices can be useful, dealing with the demands of the real world is where a person ultimately learns the most. Mike Simms, who graduated from the Cornell School of Hotel Administration in 2000 and today owns and operates seven restaurants in Southern California, recalls his first days as a newly minted manager. "Maybe my Excel skills came in handy and I could read a P & L because I'd been taught that at school," he says. "But not until I started going off and looking for real estate and having to produce business plans and marketing plans did my education start to kick in." He doesn't consider a degree necessary for the restaurant managers he hires, but he does see value in having one. "It shows dedication," he says. "It gets you a more serious look at the job."

The library call number for hospitality and restaurant management books is 647.95, and anyone considering entering the profession should be familiar with what those shelves hold at their local branch. The National Restaurant Association's *ManageFirst: Hospitality and Restaurant Man-*

agement (Pearson) gives a good overview of the many tasks required for leading a dining establishment. Elizabeth Lawrence's *The Complete Restaurateur* (Plume) offers a thorough explanation of the subject. Christopher Egerton-Thomas's *How to Open and Run a Successful Restaurant* (Wiley) provides a more opinionated take on the subject. John R. Walker's *The Restaurant: From Concept to Operation* (Wiley) includes detailed discussion of all the subjects required for opening and ongoing success. On YouTube and online, Ryan Gromfin hosts *The Restaurant Boss*, a series of concentrated and high-energy tutorials on the nuts-and-bolts of the industry.

That's the practical aspect. The philosophical one—how to inspire the teamwork necessary in a successful restaurant—has been covered from a variety of viewpoints. Though published two decades ago, Lewis C. Forrest Jr.'s *Training for the Hospitality Industry* (Educational Institute of American Hotel & Motel Association) is still excellent in its explanation of maintaining staff standards or "coaching"—what Danny Meyer in his 2006 book *Setting the Table* (Harper Perennial) calls "correction with dignity." *Lessons in Service from Charlie Trotter*, by Edmund Lawler (Ten Speed Press) is the most thorough look at the commitment required for great guest service. The best reported books provide a realistic picture of the demands, hopes, and sometimes heartbreak of the profession. Among some of the most notable are Scott Haas's *Back of the House: the Secret Life of a Restaurant* (Berkley), a book-length profile of chef Tony Maws and his Boston restaurant Craigie On Main; Karen Stabiner's *Generation Chef: Risking It All for a New American Dream* (Avery); and David Blum's *Flash in the Pan: The Life and Death of an American Restaurant* (Simon & Schuster).

The benchmark for frontline reporting is still Anthony Bourdain's *Kitchen Confidential* (Ecco), a work that with verve, insight, and self-deprecating bravado gave confidence to many to find a place for themselves inside a restaurant's door. The chapter titled "So You Want to Be a Chef? A Commencement Address" is required reading—even if you want to be a manager. The tough conditions Bourdain described run like a theme through restaurant coverage, linking George Orwell's 1930s work *Down and Out in Paris and London* to Joseph Wechsberg's 1962 portrait of Henri Soulé, *Dining at the Pavillon*, to the discussion of current issues on the Dave Chang podcast today.

Even after reading and studying, restaurants will always be an apprenticeship business. Conditions and situations vary on every shift, and you learn from others how to execute within a free-flowing, sometimes chaotic environment. It is—you should know now—the least Socratic of businesses.

There is no measured interlude for learning a newly installed point-of-sale system: It happens when the guest has ordered and servers are standing at the glowing POS screens, their fingers hovering as they learn the position of item buttons and all the sauce-on-the-side and split order modifications. Many of the most skilled people have no formal training at all. Learn from them—how to set a tempo with your movements, how to carry twelve wine glasses without a tray, how to split the check three ways (and factor in the gift card)—and eventually you can be called a restaurant person.

It is a good group of folks to belong to. You can recognize them when they forget themselves and use safety words like "corner" or "behind" at the gym. Or when someone says "Welcome" even though they seem like just one more parent in the kids' area at the park. Frankly, it's a group of people who've developed traits more of us could adopt. Restaurant people say please and thank you. They give the right of way. They tend to deescalate tense situations. They tip well. In their own environment they're battlers for quality. They get food to the rail at the same time so an entire party eats together. Hospitality exists between the big picture value and the immediate problem, and restaurant people take pride in navigating those waters, providing authenticity and warmth with integrity, humility, and welcoming smiles.

ABOUT THE AUTHOR

Patric Kuh, who started his career cooking in restaurants, is the author of *The Last Days of Haute Cuisine*, which won a James Beard Award for Writing on Food. He was *Los Angeles* magazine's restaurant critic from 2000–2017, and has been published in *Gourmet*, *Bon Appétit*, and *Food & Wine*. He currently works as a restaurant manager in the LA area.